MW01092490

Genocide ● Library - Volume 6

OUR
CROSS

M. SALPI

Translated from the Armenian by
Ishkhan Jinbashian

H. and K. Manjikian Publications
California

2014

This book is dedicated to the memory
of the 1.5 million victims of the Genocide *(Mets Yeghern)*,
which was perpetrated by the Turkish government
and people against the Armenians during 1915-1923.

The publication of this volume is also in honor
of the countless surviving orphans of the carnage,
who performed the miracle of the rebirth
of the Armenian people.

H. and K. Manjikian Publications, California

Publisher's Cataloging-in-Publication data:
Sahakian, Aram M., 1884-1968.
Our cross / M. Salpi ;
translated from the Armenian by Ishkhan Jinbashian.
California : H. and K. Manjikian Publications, 2014.
xiii, 81 p. ; 23 cm. (Genocide Library ; v.6).
Translation of: Mer khachu.
Originally published: Paris: Veradzenunt Press, 1921.
1. Sahakian, Aram M., 1884-1968.
2. Armenian massacres, 1915-1923--Personal narratives.
3. Armenian massacres, 1915-1923--Sources.
4. Genocide--Turkey--Sources.
I. Ishkhan Jinbashian. II. Title. III. Genocide Library.

ISBN 0-9914043-6-X

Design by Ishkhan Jinbashian

Illustrations:
Opposite page: original cover art of *Mer Khachu*,
by R. Shishmanian.
Other original illustrations by Yervant Demirjian.
On the back cover: Yervant Demirjian's illustration
for the story titled "For Menon."

First Edition

Printed in the United States of America

Contents

Publishers' foreword xi

About the author xiii

Our cross 1

The stars faded 3

Under the shadow of the cross 12

Derenik 17

Yegho the woodsman 28

For Menon 38

The vanquished cross 44

Hunchbacked Manuel 49

The ravine nest 55

Eaglet 65

Other publications of the Genocide Library 81

Publishers' foreword

Our Cross, the English translation of *Mer Khachu* by M. Salpi (Aram M. Sahakian) and published in the present volume as the sixth installment of the Genocide Series, is a collection of writings about the harrowing experiences of the 1915 Genocide of the Armenians.

Based on actual events and superbly documented, *Our Cross* also abounds with lucid analyses of the psychological dimensions of the calamity and its aftermath, with the tidal waves of the Armenian nation's Great Sorrow, the 1915 Genocide, bursting forth from each sentence of the book.

Through his nine intricately composed stories, Sahakian recounts the tragedy of those who survived the Genocide yet carried on their bodies and in their souls the scars of its horrors and humiliations.

A medical doctor, Sahakian was conscripted into the Ottoman Turkish army in 1914. For almost four years, he served as a medical officer at various forts and military bases in the Dardanelles, Anatolia, Cilicia, Syria-Lebanon, Palestine, Transjordan, and the deserts of the Sinai and the Hejaz, on the Arabian Peninsula.

Sahakian's privileged position in the army allowed him to witness the physical and psychological suffering of Armenian deportees who had survived the Genocide, and, as a doctor and man of conscience, to do his utmost to help ease their pain and heal them of their ailments.

Our Cross is a deeply felt chronicle of Sahakian's experiences with and through the survivors, interspersed with his cogent, eloquent reflections on the enormity of his people's loss.

His poignant stories touch on the dire circumstances of young orphans and mothers who had lost their children; young girls and women who had been violated and left with a crushing sense of dishonor and shame; elderly people who, after witnessing the massacre of their entire families, were left to fend for themselves, hopeless and without a roof over their heads; heartbroken parents who in vain searched for their abducted daughters; survivors who were forced to convert to Islam and had to carry on with a profound sense of guilt, yearning only to be buried one day with a cross on their graves; and so many other deportees who grappled with a host of nameless agonies.

During a battle while he served on the Arabian Peninsula, Sahakian was captured by the British and became a prisoner of war. But this turn of events would have a positive consequence, as he was eventually appointed resident doctor at Port Said's Armenian refugee camp, which was established by the British and French forces.

Beginning in 1918, Sahakian went beyond the call of duty to help meet the needs of Armenian refugees. His work at the Port Said refugee camp both gave him a renewed sense of purpose and an impetus to chronicle his extraordinary experiences, since 1915, as a witness of the tribulations of Genocide survivors.

It was only after moving to France that Sahakian had the opportunity to edit his writings and publish them, in 1921, as the book titled *Mer Khachu*.

Written in an elegant style brimming with the astute observations of a man of wisdom, *Mer Khachu* brings further evidence of *Mets Yeghern* as an indisputable act of genocide, thereby condemning Turkey as a genocidal state. We are proud to present the English translation of Sahakian's masterwork in the run-up to 2015, the centenary of the Armenian nation's great cataclysm.

Hagop Manjikian
June 2013

About the author

Aram M. Sahakian, whose works were published under the pen name M. Salpi, was a writer, journalist, political activist, and physician.

Born in Gamarag Village, Kesaria (Kayseri) in 1884, Sahakian was educated at Kesaria's Saint Garabed Monastery Zharankavorats School, from which he graduated in 1906. He went on to receive a medical degree from the French University of Beirut and became known as Doctor Salpi.

In 1914, at the onset of the First World War, Sahakian was conscripted into the Ottoman army, in which he served as a medical officer.

After being captured by the British, he became a prisoner of war and was taken to Port Said, Egypt.

However, in 1918, he was appointed resident doctor of a newly set up local Armenian refugee camp.

Throughout his service at the camp, Sahakian witnessed the plight of Armenian refugees and Genocide survivors from Musa Dagh and elsewhere.

A highly gifted writer, Sahakian has published his impressions of those days in two books, *Alyagner yev Khelyagner (Waves and Wrecks)* and *Mer Khachu (Our Cross)*, which present powerful, deeply moving portrayals of survivors.

Following the Armistice in 1918, Sahakian became a contributor to the newspapers *Azadamard* and *Jagadamard*, in Istanbul.

He later moved to France, where he published *Mer Khachu*, in 1921.

In 1922, he settled down in Romania, where he led the local Armenian Clinic and provided free healthcare to indigent Armenian refugees.

Doctor Sahakian also provided free healthcare to a large number of Soviet prisoners of war during the Second World War.

Sahakian died in Constanta, Romania, in 1968.

Knar Manjikian

Sources

Suren Kolanjyan, *Haykakan Sovetakan Hanragitaran*, volume 10, 1984, Yerevan.

Garo Kevorkian, *Amenun Darekirku*, 1967-1968, Beirut.

OUR CROSS

Dedicated to my martyred friends,
with whom I shared
the path of ideals and literature.

The stars faded

The evening kicked off in raucous merriment.

Although we weren't drinkers per se, glasses of arak were downed one after the other.

We talked, laughed, recalled long-lost loves, and sometimes made wishes, only to follow them with curses that were unleashed in barely restrained rage. In short, we all needed to lighten up a bit.

It was a Sunday in July 1916. Having obtained leave from our respective battalions in nearby villages, we converged at a café on the side of a brook in Zahleh, Lebanon, sitting around a table under a walnut tree. Pentecost was the ostensible occasion. In truth, we were there simply to enjoy one another's company, as old friends who had reunited through a fickle stroke of luck.

We were all guests in that land, and only for a few days: one of us was on his way to the Sinai, another was granted permission to travel to Hejaz, yet another braced himself for the torturous trek to the Caucasus he was about to embark on with his battalion. We were yesterday's survivors, now on the move again among murderous hordes, into the paths of fire and privation, having as our only refuge the prospect of an uncertain, crushing future.

There were seven of us, all Armenian exiles — including four doctors and a very young, heartbroken monk, the lone survivor among his fellow cenobites, all of whom had been slaughtered during the destruction of their monastery. Now, with his beard shaven, the monk dragged the life of a fugitive from one city to the next. Also among us was a vivacious, extremely handsome young man by the name of Hrand, who worked for the local rail company.

As the copious waters of the brook flowed through stones in a soothing gurgle, we sang at the top of our lungs, cracked jokes, and kept raising our glasses.

Following the noon heat, the air had cooled down somewhat, and the evening's purplish-red shafts of light kissed the crests of the trees.

Perhaps we did drink too much, but getting inebriated was decidedly the order of the day. The breeze, full of spellbinding exhilaration, brought zestful fragrances from afar, and the dream of blissful days, with its irresistible yearnings, once again rose in our hearts.

Ah, we were human after all! There are moments of euphoria when, if only for an instant, the mind forgets the devastation, the incalculable depth of its grief, and its relentless nightmare, and instead, ceding to a mysterious enchantment, leaves behind the brutality of circumstance in order to be transported far, quite far, in a cavorting soar.

This was the beauty of the dream, engendered by the sweetness of nature's breath, which drew us, took us to ethereal realms, where life was but a voluptuous trance and voices formed a delightful harmony.

The effects of the arak were fading slowly, imparting a sweet torpor to our fibers, as we celebrated a distinct moment, the sumptuous miracle of our dead yet reawakening lives, giddy with joy.

And by the side of that brook, sitting almost hidden beneath the extremely low-hanging branches of that walnut tree, we were possessed of a heart-rending, childlike state of euphoria as we drew one another's attention to a sliver of horizon, which, with its purple hues and ensconced in an undulating mist, seemed to have assumed the form of an enormous bird, holding a bouquet of light in its beak and carrying love's miracle to the blue skies.

Who has ever been able to accurately paint the whimsical harmony of the infinite plays of light? We cannot paint, but can well watch and feel them. And watch and feel them we did, until their intensity subsided completely. Thus, after being the accidental spectators of the joyous unwinding of our nerves, for a few hours perhaps, now we were all quiet, fallen into a bittersweet daze. Seemingly having forgotten our sorrows, carried away by nature's entrancing magic, we proceeded to muse about a paradise lost; about our hearths of old, around which life once chirped and the innocent laughter of the Armenian boy rollicked; about our fields, where the ploughman labored under a peaceful sun; and about our vineyards, where the Armenian girl sang, briskly, vibrantly, a blossoming rose made flesh underneath her headscarf.

In short, our lights of yesteryears, reemerging desires, and cherished loves paraded one by one before us as we floated in a nameless rapture,

as though the monstrous calamity of our nation had been nothing but a bad dream.

This was the miracle-seeking self-deception of disconsolate hearts in a moment of intoxication, striving desperately to open a pathway where we could find a shred of sunshine to warm our frozen longings. The trickery of sentiment was the work of an instant. But could it be perpetuated?

By then our revelry was already melting away, soon to die like the rays of sunlight at dusk. Someone made a funny comment, but it fell into silence as if it were cold lead. There was no response.

"I haven't heard from my mother in three months," suddenly said one of the doctors."

"Neither have I..."

"Me neither..."

"My mother was murdered," said a fourth voice.

"Mine was converted to Islam," said a fifth.

"Last I heard from my mother, she was in Katma," said a sixth. "Afterwards she must've gotten lost in the desert."

"Mine has died of hunger," lamented our seventh companion and broke into sobs.

We were taken aback, as we had never thought of him as prone to emotional outbursts. Clearly alcohol had weakened his nerves, making him weep like a child — and seem rather ridiculous around the arak table, despite the patent immensity of his heartache.

A few of us hastened to comfort him, as though our own sorrows hurt any less, and, in order to make our words of solace more effective, recounted some horrendous episodes from the massacres — next to which our friend's woe would seem almost trivial.

"Listen to me," one young exile said, "compare your grief to the much bigger loss of someone else and console yourself. If your mother died of hunger, at least she didn't have to live in dishonor."

Afterwards the threads began to unravel. We took turns to tell one or two eyewitness accounts of the mass killings and other atrocities, as the company listened in utter silence.

Darkness had fallen, and with it a somber heaviness blanketed our spirits, lending a gloomy harshness to our faces, which had turned pale beneath the dull light of a lantern hanging from the café's grapevine.

Our dour recollections would perhaps bear down on us still had not a certain development enter the equation, transforming the mood around the tables.

Just when we were lost in somber thought, having become brothers in our shared predicament, we noticed a young woman on the opposite side of the brook slowly walking toward us. She must've been one of the thousands of hungry beggars who were physically and spiritually crushed along the deportation routes, whom the war and the savagery of the Turk had caused to end up amid the cheerful mountains of Lebanon.

She approached our table with hesitation, as her tattered, blue frock undulated with the gentle evening breeze. The leaves of the grapevine also quivered while shadows created by the lantern's light rippled across the flagstone floor.

As she reached our table and stood before us, her eyes suddenly dilated with fear, and the words of a beggar's supplication, which obviously she had been preparing to speak, remained frozen on her half-open lips.

Her cheeks scorched by the sun. Her timorous yet fiery eyes, glistening with a striking pristine beauty, commanded her face. She looked exquisite in her fear-stricken silence, this mountain vagabond, who now, petrified beneath the lantern, found it unable to utter a single word.

"You're lovely, sis," one of our friends told her in Arabic. "You look like a doe who has escaped from the woods of Mount Sannin."

"She's a blue bird who doesn't sing anymore," said another in Armenian.

"She looks like a night fairy with three stars on her forehead," put in a third.

At this, all eyes turned to the three blue stars tattooed between the arched eyebrows of the girl.

Three or four of the men exclaimed, almost in unison: "She's really beautiful... and she's got stars on her forehead."

She was terribly embarrassed and tears began to well up in her eyes. Suddenly she turned around, darted off to the small bridge, and vanished into the night's shadows.

We all looked at one another in astonishment, as we found such an eruption of sensitivity and bashfulness on the part of a vagrant night girl rather odd, considering, naturally, that it was not some frivolous curiosity that had driven her to loiter around the arak tables.

That's when we all seemed dumbfounded, as the many questions in our shocked gazes grappled for answers. We couldn't quite explain what we experienced at that moment, but the feeling which made our hearts race was one and the same.

Perhaps we were tormented by the sense of having been unwittingly offensive toward a saintly girl, and the realization that, far from being a woman of pleasure, the tearful girl who had disappeared into the shadows was one among our nation's hundreds of thousands of wretched girls who now sought the night to conceal their shame, as they were left with no other option but to beg for a piece of bread.

Our state of shock lingered for quite a while.

"No," someone finally broke the silence. "We were fooled by her blue frock and the stars on her forehead. We should've guessed that those sad and intense eyes were of us — could be *only* of us."

"She was Armenian!" we chimed in one after the other, pouring into that cry the full measure of our distress.

But while the commotion gradually fizzled into the babble of the brook, we sank even deeper into our melancholy.

"The evening has been poisoned," someone added. "Our people's grief and shame came to find us even here. Come on, let's go find her. Maybe she'll tell us something about herself, share her grief."

"Let's go," others joined in.

Four men at once jumped to their feet and scuttled after the girl. Within a moment, we could hear their anxious screams from the other side of the brook: "Hrand, go left!" "My friend, you go up that way!"

Our low spirits now quashed the last sprouts of happiness which we desperately had wished to experience that evening, against the backdrop of a black past and an uncertain future. In vain had we believed alcohol would do the trick.

The poor monk nervously mumbled a song as the rest of us sat in tense stillness, anticipating the return of our companions and the beautiful girl.

We didn't have to wait long.

"As soon as I saw her, I had a feeling she was one of our own," said Hrand, who accompanied the girl back to our table, along with the other men.

We were speechless. We just helplessly watched our compatriot, who, now leaning against the trunk of the grapevine and with her hands cupping her face, wept bitterly.

"Please don't cry," the monk told the girl, himself gripped by emotion. "This is the Armenian's way of the cross. All we can do now is struggle, go on living, in order to dedicate our last heartbeats to our homeland. There's no dishonor, nothing to be ashamed of."

But the girl continued to cry. Neither the monk's nor our words of consolation could ease her pain.

"Let her get it out of her," Hrand said in a trembling voice. "We have to respect her suffering."

"Listen," Hrand continued, his voice rising. "As we were walking back, she gave me a little glimpse of her tragic story. Her name is Varsenig. She's from Brusa. She has lost her parents and brother during the deportations. Then she was marched off to the Syrian desert. She has made it here from godforsaken Homs. Along the way, she has changed many hands, each time managing to escape from her captors. Those tattooed stars on her forehead… they're the marks of her last master."

It was not the misfortune of Varsenig alone that tore us asunder. All of us had loves ones — mothers, sisters — who were uprooted from our ancestral lands. Where were they now?

"Now let us try to think a bit clearly," the monk said. "Our celebration turned into mourning. But let's not be carried away by dark thoughts. They serve no purpose but to break our will and weaken our inner strength. Let us instead carry on like men who have tasted adversity yet possess the vigor to live and overcome things. Let us think of how we can be of help to this poor girl."

Indeed, we had not yet had a chance to consider this, devastated as we were by Varsenig's story. We gazed at one another cluelessly. Yes, where was she supposed to go from here?

It was at that point that Varsenig spoke at last, with her clear, sonorous voice echoing against the stillness of the night.

"Don't you worry about me, my brothers," she said. "I'm a forever lost, dishonored girl. The nights feed me and cover my shame."

"No, my girl," the monk replied. "You're a treasure that has reached us by chance. Through you we remember our vanished sisters and mothers."

"What if we take her to a convent, make a donation, and ask the nuns to have her live with them for a while?" said one of the doctors.

"That's one naïve suggestion," another countered. "The Turkish government has just issued an order forbidding citizens to shelter Armenian exiles. The nuns will surely refuse to give Varsenig refuge."

"Then let's take her with us," someone said. "If our battalion gets stationed in a city, it will be easy for us to provide for her and make sure she's safe."

"We're going to Hejaz," said one of the doctors.

"We're off to the Sinai," another added.

"And we're headed to the Caucasus," put in a third, in an anxious tone.

As for the monk and his companions, they were fugitives and scarcely managed to eke out a living. They were, therefore, unable to help Varsenig.

That left Hrand, the rail worker, on whom our gazes were now unwittingly fixed. He lowered his eyes in embarrassment and confusion.

"What do you think, Hrand?" suddenly thundered the monk's voice, as though extending a ceremonial invitation to self-sacrifice.

"I think, Father," a quivering Hrand began after having let it all sink in, "that if the young lady approves, if my friends don't blame me for it, and if they promise not to make any inappropriate comments, you should wed us at this very instant. Before God and you, I promise to take care of her as my lawful wife, and give her all my affection to help her forget her pain and shame."

We all held our breaths as we listened to the astounding words of this noble youth.

Barely a second later, Varsenig threw herself at Hrand's feet and begged tearfully: "No, my brother, don't be a fool!" she entreated. "I'm a dishonored girl who's been passed from hand to hand in the desert. My body, my every fiber, is a nest of disgrace. It's filled with the contamination of savages. Spare yourself! Your generosity kills me…"

But Hrand remained silent, clearly unshakable in his resolve. Neither any of the rest of us was about to consider Varsenig's plea.

Indeed, at that moment, all one could feel was the quiver of fascination electrifying one's being. Hrand, that skinny, unassuming young man, grew in stature, became larger than life before our eyes. Against the backdrop of the unrelenting gloom and demoralization that had become our lot, all of a sudden we were catapulted into a state of consummate exultation, once again experiencing the irrepressible spirit and vitality of our people.

We all stood up mechanically and rushed to hug Hrand.

"Well done, my brother," someone said.

There were many more exclamations of praise, heartfelt words that found a deathly-pale Hrand shuddering beneath the grapevine.

Next, possessed of a mad rush of exhilaration, we tossed the arak bottles into the brook, wiped the table clean, transformed it into an "altar," and, notwithstanding Varsenig's hesitation, had her and Hrand stand before it, side by side . The ceremony could start. The monk took out a cross — a vestige of happier times — from his pocket and began to say his prayers in a faint voice. He went on to bless the selfless young man and the lost-but-found young woman.

Once the ceremony was over, we all approached the couple and congratulated and kissed them. Varsenig was blushing, exuding a mixture of embarrassment, relief, and renewed hope.

Before we dispersed into the night, impervious to the darkness of tomorrow's road and our chests swelling with lofty sentiments, the monk told us, "My friends, there are countless Varsenigs out there. If one day we are fortunate enough to be free again, tell your far-flung brothers that the martyrdom of the Armenian woman exceeded all precedents. And tell them we need the conscious sacrifice of thousands of more Hrands."

***

A year later, on my way back from Hejaz, I ran into Varsenig and Hrand at a small, dreary train station. Their faces were lit with unadulterated bliss. Apparently the surrounding desolation and endless sands had been unable to give off a single shoot of boredom in their hearts. Varsenig's forehead was now proud and held high, while her blots of shame, those three star tattoos, had been seared into tiny scars.

"Are you happy, Hrand?" I asked.

"May God not consider our happiness excessive," he said.

"Hrand is an angel among men," Varsenig added, blushing. "We suffered too much. I believe the heavens will no longer be cruel to us."

They saw me off. As the train lurched forward, Varsenig called out, "Doctor, please write your friends and tell them I'll never forget that Pentecost night. I pray for them every day!"

If only they were alive, I thought. The monk had been betrayed by informants; the Turkish police beat him to death. Our comrades who had gone to the Caucasus front eventually died of starvation. Only my friend who fought in the Sinai was still alive. It was him I was about to join.

As the train barreled forth, the desert beamed magical flashes of light into my soul, where they glittered, shattered, and grew dark, filling me with a sense of foreboding.

1918

11

Under the shadow
of the cross

Sunk in a shabby armchair on the balcony of their new home, where I often saw her, she read constantly.

Perhaps one day the moon would grow jealous of her charm and extraordinary beauty if she weren't so pale.

The poor girl was worn out. Her face was hollowed by illness, exposing her cheekbones. Her lips were of a bluish transparency and she shuddered ceaselessly, suffering from fevers. Yet her most commanding feature were her big, delicate eyes, whose crystal clarity lent her an ethereal allure.

Her name was Vaskanush. Apart from being highly educated and a voracious reader of novels, she was also an accomplished painter. At home, they called her Vaskan.

I won't recount the tragic story of their deportation — a story which, in its various permutations, has touched every Armenian native of a land which the Turk has turned into a cauldron of crime. Instead I write about Vaskan and her family's life following their exile, in Damascus.

It must've been due to the wealth and generosity of Vaskan's family, rather than mere chance, that after somehow making it alive to Damascus following a trail of unspeakable horrors, they managed to rent a home and settle down.

Some time later, the family benefited from the largess of Syria's Red Prince, Jemal, as Vaskan's brothers were given permission to engage in commerce. They also maintained courteous relations with the prince's harem.

At a time when the terror of ongoing persecution reigned among thousands of exiled Armenians, the family converted to Islam, after much deliberation, believing the move was a wise choice in view of the day's circumstances. They all assumed Islamic names. Vaskan was renamed Khendan.

Still, their relatively comfortable situation did nothing to bring a smile to her face. On the contrary, she remained pallid, and continued to wither day by day.

Her dark eyes, with their glint of supplication and knowing pain, were quintessentially Armenian. Rarely could a pair of eyes be so profoundly expressive. It seemed to me that her entire face, her head, torso, and soul consisted solely of a pair of dark eyes, whose white expanses were a mist-filled sky in which one could at once read love, death, and an entreaty for life.

Were you to ask someone whether they knew Vaskan, I am certain they would reply, "Yes, she's the girl with those strange, big eyes."

That's because anyone who saw her for the first time would first and foremost be struck by her eyes. And when people were away from her and asked themselves what of her they had taken with them, surely the indelible image of her eyes would come to the fore and disturb their imagination.

I don't know when exactly her tuberculosis had taken hold. It didn't seem a recent development — or perhaps it was but progressed extremely fast. Her skin had thinned visibly, with layers of blue vein showing above her temples. Her tall, soaring figure was now so emaciated that, with her profuse waves of flaxen hair, she looked like a marigold gently teetering on its stem.

On doctors' orders, she was taken to Lebanon, where her ailing shadow was entrusted to one mountaintop health resort after the other. The hope was that, after inhaling the air of sunny skies, she would return to life and her breath would insist on invigorating her otherwise exquisite body.

Vaskan's Lebanese sojourn proved useless. Indeed, when she returned to Damascus, the ravages of her illness could be read ever more clearly on her face. From that day onward, she read incessantly, insatiably, sitting on the balcony. She already felt that she didn't have much to live and that the few pleasures left to her were only too ephemeral. Therefore she sought to glean vicarious pleasure from her readings, in order to take away with her at least the illusion of the thrills experienced by the heroes of the novels she devoured.

She painted frequently, and did so brilliantly. Her ingenious colorations, the product of a sensitive imagination, were a delight to behold. For she was a girl of twilight and drew inspiration from the very source. With her eyes always fixed on the magnificent skies of dusk, she ravenously took in the sorrow but also discreet joys of those moments.

"Come inside, my girl," her mother would say. "It's enough for today." Or "It's too cold outside."

"Just a bit longer, mother," Vaskan would reply. "How beautiful this sunset is!"

There came a time when her legs stopped supporting her body. Family members carried her and the little armchair she sat on to the balcony. From the moment she became unable to walk, what pained her the most was that her arms had weakened as well, with the result that she could no longer hold her beloved books.

One day, as she sat on the balcony, the rays of the vanishing sun set her skeletal face alight. Pulsating with an otherworldly beauty framed by the waves of her golden locks, she resembled a fairy.

"Daydreaming?" I asked jokingly as I approached her.

"No," she said, "I was just wondering what I look like now."

"Well, you look like a bundle of sunshine."

"Thank you," she said, smiling. "If only I could hold my brush now."

"To paint the sunset?"

"Yes," she said in a whisper. "Look at those magical hues... Today, more than ever, I feel as if I know the meaning of life, the joy of being alive. That's because I sense the coming of death."

Her disconcerted, imploring eyes were now fixed on me.

"No, my girl, don't say such foolish things," I objected. "I swear that death will be spellbound by your eyes."

She was silent for a few minutes. At any rate, she lacked the energy to speak. Withdrawn into herself, she seemed to be carried off to distant realms unfamiliar to us.

Then she remembered something. "Doctor," she said, "the Armenian deportees are still suffering. They're dying of hunger."

"They certainly are," I said. "But you shouldn't be worrying about that. The savages have created a bloody fate for the Armenian. It's a fate that's now bound to run its course."

"I wish I could die right now for the deportees... if only that would end their pain."

Heavy is the awareness of death for a heart brimming with boundless dreams. Yet she was prepared to make the ultimate sacrifice for her compatriots.

As darkness fell, her mother came outside. "Khendan," she said, "let's go in, it's cold."

A bitter smile strained Vaskan's lips. "Doctor," she said, "I don't want to be buried as Khendan. I just wish I can have a small, white grave with a cross on top, next to a willow."

"Be quiet," her mother said. "We can't afford to have anyone hear such talk. Remember, we formally accepted the 'holy religion.'"

***

On a rainy day, Vaskan died, as do all those who are afflicted with tuberculosis.

Her family did not have a chance to grieve for her. What perturbed them, even more than the loss of their young daughter, was the thorny issue of where to bury her.

Officially they were Muslim converts. In Syria, a land of ongoing Turkish state terror, irresoluteness regarding matters of religion and religious propriety, such as burial, could be tantamount to inviting a death sentence. The family was duty-bound to invite a Muslim person to perform the ritual washing and shrouding of the virgin body. Subsequently it had to be taken to a Muslim cemetery, where it was to be lain to rest under a crescent.

They deliberated into the small hours of the night, consulted friends. They were at their wits' end.

Eventually their pangs of guilt prevailed, and they forgot the dire consequences, including persecution, exile, and death, any or all of which were certain to follow if their subsequent actions ever came to light.

They brought home a common enough wooden trunk to avoid suspicion.

They cold-heartedly and without the slightest difficulty folded Vaskan's wasted body in two and fitted it into the box. They then bribed someone to help them take the "coffin" to the Armenian cemetery, where they buried it. A few days later, they placed a cross above Vaskan's humble grave.

Barely a month had passed before the secret was out. Indeed, the news spread like wildfire, inevitably reaching also the ears of high-ranking Turkish officials and their families, many of whom were close friends of

Vaskan's family. Vaskan had drawn charcoal portraits for Jemal and Governor Tahsin.

The discovery of Vaskan's Christian burial caused quite a stir. The Turkish authorities opened an investigation into the affair, seeking to find the Armenian priest who had officiated the burial as well as every sordid detail pertaining to the "gross sacrilege."

There they were, the very monsters who had destroyed our ancestral homes and churches, massacred entire communities, and raped ten-year-old girls, now making an uproar in the name of righteousness and decorum.

My deceased, poet sister, I don't know why till this day I obstinately disregard the memory of the Turkish desecration of your hapless bones, instead imagining a spirited, enchanting girl with fair hair and dark eyes who now rests under the shade of a cross next to a willow.

1918

Derenik

It was almost dawn when at last we were able to take a respite.

The shelling, with its hellish ferocity, had gone on all night. Our poor canyon, Kereviz Dere, where we had taken shelter for the past three months, in a hollow at the base of a boulder and in several trenches nearby, was once again assaulted by relentless bombardment by the French.

Kereviz Dere was the bloodiest, most vulnerable spot of the front at Sed-ul-Bahr — a village on the shore of the Dardanelles. With the enemy positioned on top of the hill across, we were easy pickings and sustained heavy casualties on a daily basis.

Throughout the night, as the bombs fell, a Greek doctor and I tended to the injured. We also processed hundreds of corpses, hanging from their necks the red death certificates which showed the names of the deceased as well as the specific injuries that had caused their deaths.

That morning, when many of us were curled up inside our lair, after a sleepless night, we had a visitor. It was a very young officer, who, like anyone else coming inside, had to bend his head and torso down to his waist in order to squeeze in through the tiny opening which served as the door of our cave.

"What do you want?" I asked.

"I'd like to speak with Dr. S.," he said.

"That's me," I replied and invited him to sit down.

"My name is Derenik M.," he said. "For the past week, I've been meaning to come to see you, but couldn't because of the fighting. Only this morning was I able to get away. I'm stationed at Kanli Dere. I very much would like to discuss with you some literary issues, especially regarding prose poems, which are of great interest to me."

I was stunned.

"Are you sick in the head?" I asked.

"Why do you say that?" he wondered.

"There should be a limit to insolence, don't you think, son? After a night of heavy bombardment, just when we've finally gotten a chance to sleep it off a bit, frankly, this ill-timed music of yours sounds lame in the extreme. Do you want to know what literature is in these parts, among these rocks? It's about blood, son. And certain death. Now I suggest you go back and just forget about literature."

He stood up, visibly insulted, said a curt goodbye, and rushed out of the cave.

After he left, I realized how terribly rude I'd been. Yet I merely shrugged my shoulders, by way of expressing remorse, and once again plunged my head into my pillow.

"Literature?" I repeated to myself. "Really? We haven't slept in two days, and this imbecile dreams of prose poems from the trench..."

I didn't see the "poet boy" again for some time. Only on a few occasions, when I was out visiting the front trenches, I heard officers praise a young sergeant called Derenik. I learned that he had completed his training in a mere six months at the Junior Officers' College (which had been created at the onset of the war), and had the misfortune of being sent, at the first opportunity, to the Sed-ul-Bahr line.

For extraordinary bravery and the audacious raids which Derenik and his platoon had pulled off during the clashes of July 25, 1915 — which were to come to be known as the most horrific of the Battle of the Dardanelles — he had received a special commendation. Moreover, a black-and-white German ribbon was added to the red-and-white one on his chest.

Some two months after our meeting, on a sunny August day, Derenik reappeared at the entrance of our cave. He had a slight shrapnel injury on his right arm.

While dressing his wound, I intently watched his childlike, handsome face, which was stern and unperturbed, as though he went to great lengths to make his countenance worthy of the seriousness and dark aura of a sullen, 40-year-old man. As for his fiery, dark eyes, they worked hard to leave an impression of aloofness, and remained aimlessly focused on the rocks across. Yet I could instantly notice, within his hard-to-conceal fumbling manner, the air of a boy who was cross with me.

In those moments, I so loved this innocent face that I had an older brother's urge to hold his cheeks, kiss his forehead, and say a few heartfelt words to win his heart back.

I couldn't. Was it my sense of propriety? Was it pride?

The young sergeant's face was so severe that at first I considered it pointless, and perhaps a tad humiliating for me, to start a conversation. But then I reminded myself that he was but a boy, barely 20, who had been plucked from his school desk without being allowed to savor the joys of his life's spring, and then was tossed here, among a horde of boorish soldiers, who shared absolutely nothing with his mind, heart, and spirit.

"Derenik, were you hurt by what I said that day?" I asked gently.

He turned his fierce eyes to me, giving me a rancorous stare.

"No," he said dourly. "Why would I be hurt?"

"Come on," I said. "Little brothers should not stay cross with their older brothers."

That's all it took. His face suddenly relaxed, with a tiny smile now wrinkling his tense features.

I didn't give him a chance to reply, as I held him by the shoulder and lightly pushed him into our lair.

"Stay here awhile," I told him. "Let me take care of the injured, and then you and I will talk at length about literature."

When I returned to the cave some time later, I found him sitting in the half-shadow, his eyes twinkling affably.

"Derenik, that day I felt awful for having treated you so harshly," I said. "I was so exhausted that I thought you were mocking me with talk about literature."

He couldn't answer, and once again a bashful smile graced his boyish face.

Suddenly in came Dikran Kassabian, a doctor who was also a renowned poet. Kassabian, whose pen name was Karun, had arrived a few days earlier, with an army division from Izmir. After some small talk, Kassabian took out a small notebook from his pocket and read aloud a passionate poem which he had written inspired by a centuries-old olive tree next to his previous encampment. (Incidentally, Kassabian was to meet a tragic end on the Galician front).

How baffling the human heart is! Outside, only a few steps from us, cadavers dotted the landscape, critically injured soldiers moaned with indescribable pain, and, from one instant to the next, death could sound its alarm to us as well. Yet we, whose fingers carried the perpetual traces of blood, went on musing about life's beauty and conjured up the loftiest of images. Oblivious to the carnage outside, and despite the horrific din of discharging canons and exploding shells, we relished the breath of tranquility which accompanied the "song" of the olive tree, reveling in our renewed yearnings for life and love.

After Kassabian finished reading, I introduced Derenik to him in more detail.

"Karun," I said, "in his trench, Derenik is the very spirit of audacity. But it seems he's not satisfied with the sword alone; he's also a great devotee of literature."

Then I asked Derenik, "When will we read your prose poems?"

His face turned red, and he gazed at me like someone caught with his finger in the cookie jar.

"How do you know I've written prose poems?" he asked.

"I'll bet that you have a neat notebook where you meticulously copy your poems — the pieces you get the chance to write during lulls in the trench, against the monotony of fighting, while waiting for the next attack."

"Was it Hamdi who told you?"

"My naïve boy!"

I then asked him to come visit us as often as possible, on the pretext of needing to have his wound tended, and told him I would be delighted to always be his friend.

***

Thereafter Derenik dropped in almost every day. He also loosened up, albeit slowly, coming to realize that our cave could be a warm corner for heart-to-heart exchanges, and that my brotherly feelings toward him were entirely genuine. Indeed, he trusted me enough to give me his notebook one day, asking me to read his poems and comment on them.

I started reading as soon as he had gone.

His writings began with beautiful, ornately decorated initials, which were a nostalgic throwback to elementary school. The titles of his pieces, which, with few exceptions, were followed by the designation "Prose Poem" in parentheses, were decidedly operatic: "A Fete of Blood," "The War Cry," "The Cadavers," and so on.

The poems themselves were short and lovely, the sentiments he conveyed often a bit too dramatic and delicate. Overall, the style was affected, burdened with a surfeit of precious words— the work of a novice.

When Derenik came back the next day, I told him I was impressed by the depth of his feelings, but suggested, with utmost tact, that his poems could be much more effective and sound more natural if they weren't so florid. I went on to give him some basic tips for writing in a simpler vein. He was quite receptive, given his belief that writing was his proper calling — even if it seemed to me that his most salient gift lay in being a noble and fearless warrior.

Derenik swelled with pride every time I called him "Little Poet."

As the war continued, claiming dozens, sometimes hundreds, of lives every day, Derenik was ever on the lookout for fresh themes and topics among the dead, even though he often repeated himself. I gently brought the latter fact to his attention and added that he could do well to leave aside the bloody episodes of war for a while and instead write about his far-away home, childhood, loves, and dreams — subjects which could assume extraordinary poignancy in view of his loneliness and the imminent danger of death.

"But how do you know I have loves and dreams?" he asked.

"Well, I'm pretty sure you have a poet's feelings for a girl, whose eyes are blue — or at least you've turned them blue for the purposes of your writings. Then there should be two or three other girls for whom you harbor various feelings: romantic love, affection, desire. In other words, feelings which perturb your hours in the trench as you wait for the next round of fighting."

He gazed ahead, pensive and confused. It seemed he was making a mental list of the girls he knew or desired, by way of verifying what I had just told him.

"Don't bother, my Little Poet," I said. "You know I'm right. If tomorrow you bring me your other notebook, the one in which your loves are sung, we'll have more reasons to discuss your prose poems. Without love, a tender and sensitive soul such as yours would be like nettles sprouting on the side of a river."

***

The French had managed to build a blockhouse to the far left of us, toward the seashore. Through this offensive strong point, they constantly threatened to compromise our left wing, something which would allow them to gain control of our rear positions and endanger our first line of trenches.

For months, this unimpressive-looking blockhouse, which the French built with nothing but sandbags and manned with no more than five soldiers at a time, became the living nightmare of the Turkish commanders. The Turks sent out one elite force after the other to capture the structure. But every time the Turkish troops drew close, the French troops quickly withdrew to the hills, from which those terrible bombs rained down mercilessly on the attackers.

Hundreds of soldiers perished trying to seize the blockhouse. Whenever it was damaged by a Turkish attack, the French rebuilt it during the night, so that by morning we were once again faced with the eyesore, which came to be known as our "red terror."

One evening, Derenik came running to the cave. He said he had obtained permission to lead a charge on the blockhouse under cover of darkness. This time the plan was not to try to capture but rather obliterate it, if only for the symbolism.

"Derenik, aren't you afraid?" I asked.

"Oh, no, I think we'll be fine," he said. "My heart is racing with excitement. Once we get this done, I'm thinking I'll write a fervent, blood-soaked poem about the experience."

"Blood-soaked indeed! You crazy boy, don't you give any thought to the possibility of losing your life in the process?"

Apparently he didn't. He gazed intently at me for a moment, then said, "Perhaps I should. But I never think of death because I've got such a strong desire to live."

He then said goodbye and vanished into the canyon.

I was dejected. There he was, I thought, a vivacious youth, with such promise, about to haughtily and naively risk his life for an inconsequential moment of glory.

But just as I was trying to make sense of it all, Derenik suddenly reappeared, this time looking somber and brooding.

"What," I said jokingly, "did you forget your prose poems?"

"I've been thinking that I might die tomorrow," he said as he sat down. "I must confess, it's a bit unsettling. So I came back to say some things I haven't told you before."

"So here it goes," he went on. "I don't have a father. I've got a mother and three sisters, and I love them very much. My sisters are married. Should something happen to me, I think they'll find consolation in their own families. But my mother... She won't be able to handle it."

"Just be careful out there and don't lose your will to live," I advised.

"Well, that's a given. But let's be realistic. If I don't make it alive, please don't forget about my mother. I'd like you to be kind enough to do for her some things which fate might prevent me from doing myself. And then there are my prose poems. I keep them in my little box in our trench. My whole soul is in those poems."

"It certainly is…" I said.

He left in high spirits.

The raid which Sergeant Derenik and his platoon carried out was an unprecedented success. They penetrated the French blockhouse just before dawn, took four French soldiers prisoner, and blew up the hated structure.

Subsequently, as the French staggered under our relentless fire, it took them four harrowing days to rebuild the blockhouse. This might seem an insignificant span of time, but we were at war, and four days of having the upper hand was by no means a negligible achievement.

Derenik was widely praised among officers and troops alike as a bona fide hero.

***

I next saw Derenik some three weeks later.

"Brought some new poems, did you?" I asked with a smile.

"No," he said. "That's all finished for me."

He was pale, melancholy, with none of the former glow of the innocent, happy boy to grace his face.

"What's wrong?" I asked.

"I hadn't received a single letter in the past two months," he said. "I got one today. The Turks have deported my mother."

"Mine too," I said.

We stared at one another by way of finishing our thoughts. At that moment, Derenik grew, became a man, and we became one in spirit, brothers in our shared sorrow.

"Alas!" he broke the silence at last as he stood up. "I have devoted my life and blood to this filthy homeland."

With that, he tore both of his ribbons of valor off his chest, crumpled them, and tossed them into the putrid, muddy waters of the trench outside the cave. "Those things have been searing my chest," he said.

"I understand only too well," I said.

Then, holding out a small bundle of papers, he announced, "Here's the last one. It's my last poem, and I've dedicated it to you."

I accepted the bundle with a deep sense of sympathy. I had a feeling this last work of his contained the entire tragedy, and despondency, of his broken young soul.

That evening, despite my entreaties and the torrent of exploding shells and flying shrapnel, Derenik calmly ambled toward his trench. What was death to him at this juncture?

His last poem was a tender, heart-rending tribute to his mother. As I read the piece, with my eyes welling up with tears, I lamented the loss of my own mother.

And something else: I realized that Derenik had been developing into a most sensitive and accomplished poet all along, and that perhaps the terrible news about his mother had functioned as the critical turning point for his maturation. I felt remorse for having poked gentle — and at times not so gentle — fun at his earnest enthusiasm for his craft.

***

To the right of us sat a small mound known as Ghazi Tepe, for the conquest of which close to 30,000 soldiers had lost their lives. The British had managed to build a trench there, and used it to hurl grenades at our trenches. We were determined to blow up the mound for some much-needed respite and a measure of strategic advantage.

We had begun digging a tunnel for some time. The plan was to push the tunnel all the way to the bottom of the mound and dynamite it. We had reached the halfway point. But then panic struck our quarters, as our German engineer discovered that the British had been digging a tunnel of their own, toward us, and were fast approaching our positions — he could hear the faint sounds of pickaxes from the other side.

There was no time to waste. We needed to blow up the tunnel at the point we had reached, before the British could dig into our side of the battle line and do what we were intent on doing to them.

The German engineer placed over 200 kilos of dynamite at the far end of the tunnel and secured the explosives with a heavy metal door.

In the meantime, Derenik and another sergeant were given a platoon and stood ready to attack, in order to quickly capture the crater that was expected to open up following the explosion.

While the majority of our troops were positioned in the trenches, the officers, among them myself, stood at a distance to watch what was about to unfold. The detonation order was given a little before sunset.

An instant before we heard the hellish explosion, a horrific sheet of fire ripped through our trench. Then the ground shook and produced a massive column of smoke, and a downpour of earth and stone descended on our heads.

In the ensuing pandemonium, as we instinctively ducked for cover, many of us looked at each other in utter astonishment. What could have possibly gone wrong?

The news spread soon enough: in his haste, the German engineer had failed to properly secure the dynamite door, with the result that the brunt of the explosion had struck our own trenches, instantly killing and injuring hundreds.

As if this were not enough, the British, mistaking the explosion for an offensive on our part, had begun to open fire on our troops. Our dazed soldiers, with ears ringing and dust blinding their eyes, became human fodder for the British sharpshooters.

I bolted to our cave. Just before reaching it, I saw a few injured soldiers and a sergeant who limped and crawled toward me, desperate for medical attention. The sergeant was Derenik's comrade-in-arms. Also joining us was our commander, who offered some nervous words of consolation to the wounded.

Just then, we noticed three gravely injured men close by in the ravine. As the commander and I rushed to offer help, I recognized one of them. It was Derenik. Lying on the ground in a pool of blood, he had the color of death about him.

My heart sank.

His right leg was missing, and there were shrapnel holes throughout his body. He was covered with earth and blood.

He recognized me. His fading eyes lit up a bit, but he couldn't talk. The soldier standing next to him explained that while Derenik and his detachment waited by the frontline trench, ready to attack, a bullet struck him on the shoulder. When they rushed him toward the cave to have his wound tended, shrapnel from a bomb that had fallen close by sheared off his leg and lacerated the rest of his body.

Deeply moved, our commander bent down and told him, "Derenik, my son, don't you worry, you're going to be fine."

Derenik gazed at the Turkish commander for several seconds. Then, managing to move his hands a bit, he gathered enough strength to speak, as though in meditation. "Turks," he said, "for God's sake, look after my mother."

At that moment, a soldier screamed at the top of his lungs, "Black cat coming!"

The "black cats" were the enormous shells which we could see go up in the air from the enemy side. When they rose to a certain altitude, it was possible to more or less determine their target. If your position happened to be the bomb's aim, there was only one thing to do: run like hell.

As we attended to Derenik's wounds, we saw clearly that the incoming "black cat" was headed straight for us.

The terror of the fiery monstrosity sent us scurrying. No sooner had we taken cover beneath a boulder that the shell exploded with a deafening thunder.

Seconds later, as the clouds of smoke and earth thinned out, I ran to Derenik. This time, however, what remained from the young poet was a blood-soaked, severely mutilated jumble of flesh, like a final, devastating poem.

***

Two years later, when I was in Aleppo, not a soul among the hundreds of exiles I inquired with knew anything about Derenik's mother. Then, one day, while visiting a friend, I met an Armenian young woman who worked as a maid at the home of a Turkish aristocrat from Derenik's hometown. She was a Genocide survivor who was simply appropriated by the Turkish bey for her beauty and youth. Once again, I made inquires, and was overjoyed to discover that she was an acquaintance of Derenik's mother, whose story she proceeded to tell me.

After surviving the massacres, Derenik's mother had ended up in Aleppo's Karluk district. She was emaciated and destitute, and died shortly of starvation.

Imagine that: the mother of a war hero who had been decorated by the Ottoman Turkish and German armies alike, who had fought with extraordinary bravery and fallen on the battlefield, had died of hunger. The Turks had not outright murdered Derenik's mother "in the name of Allah." Rather, they had been "kind" enough to let her waste away on the streets of Aleppo.

1918

Yegho the woodsman

To a dear friend, Dr. K.

He had stuffed a few pounds of bulgur, a palmful of olives, and some lavash bread in his calico bundle, which was patched together with pieces from old garments.

On a Sunday morning, Yegho the woodsman stood by the rickety fence of his small house to say goodbye to family and neighbors.

"Brother, there's a dearth of black among your hair," an old friend told Yegho. "Had they gotten your birth date right in those registers of theirs, who would've thought of drafting you?"

Without kissing his wife, Yeghsa, or embracing his children — Vartug, Mariam, Simon, and Mardig — who clung to their mother's skirt, the middle-aged Yegho reluctantly began to walk toward the canyon below, leaving his ancestral village behind, heading out to faraway Golgothas, his rough features contorted with an uncharacteristic mixture of despondency and confusion.

One of the Genocide's most heart-rending chapters pertains to the countless thousands of Armenian conscripts in the Ottoman Turkish army who were relegated to hard labor. Unarmed, malnourished, and almost naked, these men worked 18 hours a day in snow or rain, or under a scorching sun, along desolate roads or in deserts, only to be massacred down the line, or left to succumb to starvation or disease.

Yegho began to labor alongside his compatriots in the Dardanelles. Their quarters consisted of a string of tattered tents, in which they were allowed to sleep no more than five hours a night.

They had to be up and gather around just before dawn, carrying their picks and shovels. They were then marched in single file for several hours, until they reached this or that remote location, where they had to repair trenches, break rocks, or build roads. They worked almost nonstop, and

were whipped promptly by their Turkish taskmasters for the slightest attempt at a respite. Perhaps the worst of it was that they had to toil away in utter self-denial, for a homeland which had been "merciful" enough to spare their lives, "benevolent" enough not to smash their heads with axes, for a while at least, since they were deemed useful for the war effort.

Following the Dardanelles tragedy, the Turkish army did not outright slaughter Yegho's battalion — whereas, after months of hard labor, thousands upon thousands of Armenian conscripts from throughout Turkey were mass-murdered by firing squad, on direct orders of the Turkish government. Instead Yegho's battalion was marched to the Sinai Desert, where the Turks proceeded to literally work the men to death, in unspeakably inhumane conditions.

***

Some 20,000 of Yegho's group, the 18th Labor Battalion, perished in the Sinai. By 1917, no more than 150 souls were left alive. They were but wraiths by that time, emaciated beyond recognition, barely resembling human beings, yet with a supplicating, moist, sweet fire in the depth of their eyes, the universal imprint of the Armenian victims.

Eventually thousands more were added to the surviving conscripts in the Sinai. The Turkish army had hunted them down across the mountains and valleys of Western Armenia, or yanked them away from deportee caravans, and marched them to the desert. By the time they reached their final destination, these once-vigorous men invariably suffered from starvation or disease, and often both.

I can never forget the solicitous eyes of the old Armenian pharmacist, a native of Izmit, who ran to me every time he came across some fellow Armenians among the multitudes of ailing soldiers brought to Jerusalem's Russian hospital.

"Doctor," he used to say, "let's try to save at least these poor folks."

There was nothing I wouldn't try for them. My assistant, Sister Teufel, rushed to their help. But all our care and compassion, our faith in our chances of defeating ruthless death, would come to naught. I had never yearned for a miracle as much I did while at the bedside of those Armenian patients. Without an exception, they were reduced to skeletons who heaved with the haste of the dying, their eyes buried deep in their sockets, soon to be frozen like a couple of glass beads.

Thus died — or rather were extinguished — the Armenians in that hospital: slowly, quietly. They simply opened their mouths for one last time, and their eyes froze in a blood-curdling gaze into space.

Yet the overwhelming majority of Armenian conscripts expired not in a hospital bed, but out in the field. Many were found dead in their tents the morning after a rainy and cold night. Numerous others, despite burning with typhus, were forced under the blows of the Turkish whips to toil in the sands, shovel in hand and bearing with haunting stoicism the cross of a martyred people. Such men were too weak to escape to a remote spot in order to die in dignity. Rather, they snuck away to the side of a brush or into a ditch, where they breathed their last breath thirsty and feverish, remembering in one last bout of idiocy the beautiful days of yesteryears and their lost hearths.

Yegho, the eldest among his battalion, was perhaps also one of the bravest, as he endured his pain with astounding forbearance, till the very end. Even the Turks, in their sneering manner, showed him respect. He never shunned work, made the best of his circumstances, and tried to comfort the young men who cursed at their fate, by offering them his fatalistic views. A devout Christian, Yegho was led by his rock-solid conviction that God metes out suffering only to replace it with profuse laughter. Every night, irrespective of the horrors he had experienced or witnessed during the day, he knelt down in his tent, said his prayers, and closed his eyes in profound contentment.

This is how Yegho spent his first year in the Sinai. He had no news of his family. On his return from the Dardanelles, while passing through Istanbul, he had heard that the Armenian community of his village, too, was uprooted and marched off to the east. His lone hope was that the Turkish authorities would have spared his family on account of his loyal service to the army. If this were the case, he thought, he could eventually return to his birthplace, where he could eke out a living as a farmer or by becoming a servant in some Turkish home.

He shared his tent with a young man by the name of Garbis, who was the son of Sarkis Agha, a wealthy businessman from Yegho's village.

Garbis was a frail youth, about 19 years old at the time. He had a pleasant, feminine face, light-brown hair, and a pair of glistening, terror-stricken eyes which exuded the meek complacence of the soon-to-be-slaughtered.

Yegho was this weak boy's self-appointed guardian angel, driven more by servile empathy than fatherly sentiment. Indeed, Yegho could not reconcile with his peasant's sense of ethics and propriety the fact that Sarkis Agha's son now found himself in such a dire predicament.

Many of the Armenian laborers thought Yegho was Garbis' father. Even the Turkish officers had noticed Yegho's devotion to the bony young man with the feminine face, who accompanied him to work. While Yegho led the way, carrying a couple of shovels and a small lunch bag, Garbis, scruffy like a beggar, dodderingly followed the elder's steps, his eyes fixed on the ground.

Who could've imagined that Yegho, that uncouth peasant, was capable of such nobleness of heart, in those terrible circumstances? His seemingly inexhaustible selflessness made the cynics, those who were given to looking down on him as a simpleton, secretly bite their fingers with envy.

With pieces of fabric he had collected from here and there, Yegho had sewn a bed for Garbis, and stuffed it with grass he had gathered from the desert. He would not let Sarkis Agha's only son, who was used to warm rooms, now toss and turn on the cold ground like a scabby dog. Often Yegho mended Garbis' socks and clothes, and without fail woke up twice every night to make sure the young man was snugly covered with his blanket.

"Oh, Lord," Yegho prayed for Garbis, "he's such a fragile bequest left to my care. I beg you to spare him."

Of course no one had entrusted that boy to his care, and not a soul from their village had an inkling of the fact that Yegho and Garbis had ended up in the same labor battalion. Yet with his overflowing tenderness, the old woodsman believed that providence itself had assigned him the task of looking after the frail young man, perhaps so that the light of their hometown's most prosperous family could be saved by the sheer strength of a tough and experienced man such as himself.

Fellow soldiers who knew otherwise often teased him. "Yegho," one of them once said, "in the days you were gathering sticks in your village, I suppose Garbis' daddy grieved for your bleeding fingers, eh!"

Yegho grumbled at such jibes. He never understood these braggarts, who didn't seem to know that the notables of a village always remained notable, having been elevated to their status by God's will, the sanctity of which demanded to be respected in sincere submission.

Karekin, a fellow townsman, brought Yegho some dreadful news one day. Almost every Armenian in their village had been axed to death. Not a single boy under the age of ten was left alive. Moreover, government-organized gangs of Turkish and Kurdish murderers had raided caravans of Armenian deportees, then forced all the young females to bare their chests in order to separate the young girls and women from the rest, take their picks, and subsequently turn them into concubines or servants.

Yegho's wife, Yeghsa, was left untouched, as she wasn't considered attractive enough. All of their children, except Vartug and Mariam, had already perished in the early days of the carnage.

Most everyone from Sarkis Agha's household was slaughtered and the girls were abducted. Only Garbis' elderly mother and a boy of five had survived. Now these two were in Kefer Soos, a village near Damascus. Reduced to abject poverty, the former matriarch subsisted on a few pennies a day, selling tobacco on the streets, with help from Yegho's wife. Thus Yeghsa walked to Damascus every day to buy small quantities of tobacco, which were then peddled by Garbis' mother.

On her way back to Kefer Soos, Yeghsa often stopped to catch her breath, standing on the side of a road, at the bazaar, or among groups of people loitering by the church or nearby neighborhoods. She could tell from their tattered clothes and supplicating gazes that they were Armenians — just like Yegho, men who were once the vigorous heads of thriving families, now crushed, demeaned, shriveled, resembling stray dogs; ghastly apparitions who avoided the sun, and, languishing under the burden of their wretchedness, ambled around at shadowy street corners.

Almost every day, Yeghsa also stopped by the train station on her way back to the village. Huddled against a wall, she watched the throngs of famished, trembling, pallid, skeletal men who disembarked and could scarcely drag their wasted bodies to a hospital. These were the sickly or wounded remnants of the Turkish army, shipped once every two days from the desert by their hundreds, in desperate need of medical care.

With eyes wide open and a pounding heart, Yeghsa made her rounds among the crowds of soldiers, hoping against hope to come face to face with Yegho. She imagined she would clutch the exhausted warrior's hands, cry tears of joy, and give him a little tobacco.

In the more than six months that she had passed through the train station, Yeghsa had heard from Armenian soldiers only some fragmentary news about her husband. Once she even received a letter from him — he assured her that he was doing well, and entreated her to teach the girls all the prayers and never to forget about God's mercy.

Karekin also said that Yeghsa had begged him to convince Yegho to find a way to come visit them in Kefer Soos, if only for a short time.

The following day, Yegho went to work with unusual vigor, as though Karekin had brought him good tidings.

***

Life in the tents went on as usual, with the number of Armenian dead rising on a daily basis.

In the meantime, the Turkish commander had formed a music band comprised of young Armenian conscripts from Izmit, Adapazari, and elsewhere. Every night, gathering around the arak table, the commander and his colleagues made merry while the Armenian musicians were ordered to play into the wee hours for the pleasure of the Turkish officers.

Back in the tents, groups of Armenian conscripts often got together at night and reminisced. They spoke of their lost families, homes, orchards, businesses, and communities, and of dreams that were cut short. Sometimes middle-aged men who told these stories fell silent in mid-sentence, unable to go on. Their faces showed not the slightest contortion and their eyes remained wide open, yet tears could be seen trickling down their cheeks. At moments like these, their emotional state would prove infectious, as other men, especially the older ones, beginning to weep quietly, in pained recognition and empathy. Nothing in my life has affected me more than the sight of a grown man crying in despair.

Still, it wasn't all tears and despondency in the tents. Once in a while, the men sang songs of the old country, while the more educated among them segued into riveting performances of Gomidas.

One night, a young conscript told the story of an encounter between an Armenian priest and a group of Turkish men.

" We were at the Haydar Pasha Train Station," he recalled. "Hundreds of Armenian deportees were shoved into a corner of the terminal, among them our priest. A few Turks ceremoniously approached him, with a creepy, sardonic smile on their faces. As if they didn't know perfectly what was happening, one of them asked the priest in a feigned tone of deep concern, like an old friend would: 'What's this about, Reverend efendi? Where are you people headed?' The priest's face darkened, and he turned his head away in irritation. He then said, 'God has died; I'm going to bury him.'"

Waves of sharp, bitter laughter rang out in the tent. But Yegho shook his head in anger. He could never forgive these loudmouths for such blasphemous impertinence.

***

Within months, the 18th Labor Battalion was all but decimated.

Then, on a wet October morning, after a particularly terrible night of feverish convulsions, Garbis was unable to get out of bed. Yegho, perhaps for the first time in his adult life, told a lie: pretending to suffer from diarrhea, he obtained from the battalion's callous Turkish doctor permission to rest for 24 hours.

That day, Yegho kept watch over the ailing young man, nursed him as would a father. He kept dipping his handkerchief in water and placing it on Garbis' forehead, made tea for him, several times, and in vain tried to find some yogurt for the patient.

The following night, Yegho himself was struck by fever. Yet despite the fire which consumed him, he never left Garbis' side, dripping drops of water on the poor boy's tongue.

Four nights later, Yegho collapsed, while Garbis barely hung on to life.

In the morning, the doctor came to their tent. He couldn't be more clinical. "The young one is too weak," he declared. "Maybe he won't last the trip to Damascus. Just leave him here. Take the other one to the train station." The verdict was clear enough: Garbis was already good as dead, like thousands before him — not even worth the trouble of sending him to a hospital.

Yegho opened his eyes in terror.

"Have mercy, doctor, in God's name," he said. "I'll get better tomorrow. Please leave me here so I can take care of the boy, I beg you."

"Shut up, idiot!" the doctor screamed. "You'll go, he'll stay, and that's that."

He then turned to the soldier standing next to him, and, pointing at Yegho, "Take this dog out of here right now," he said.

⁕⁕⁕

The reason that some 300 patients, including Yegho, were being transported to Damascus was that hospitals in Jerusalem were already full. The situation was even more dire in Nazareth, where over 200 sick or injured soldiers lay on the sides of streets.

Each of the train's wagons, designed to accommodate 40 people, was packed with 80. The stench was unbearable. Then there were the heart-rending moans of the sick and dying, who kept begging for a drop of water, to no avail. There was not a single nurse, let alone a physician, on-board. People died in their dozens. Whenever someone expired, his body was simply tossed aside.

The train reached Damascus on a rainy evening. A Christian doctor came aboard to examine the new arrivals while a few donkey carts stood ready outside. He went from one wagon to the next, took a quick look at each man, and shot orders accordingly.

Yegho was unable to move. A couple of men pulled him by the legs and slid him out. "He's in bad shape," the doctor decided and approved him as a hospital patient.

In the pounding rain, a soldier carried Yegho to one of the carts.

Shaking uncontrollably, he remained stretched out on the wooden planks for quite a while. The cart was to fill up with other patients before it could be driven to one of the city's hospitals.

In the meantime, a woman stood by the cart, looking intently at the old soldier, hesitating to come closer. It was Yeghsa.

The man in the cart was scruffy and gaunt, with protruding bones, an overgrown mustache and beard, and skin the color of lead. But there was no mistaking his eyes: the same large, kind eyes which jutted out of the shadow of his thick brows. It had to be Yegho.

He turned to her. They recognized each other at once.

"Woman, is that you?" Yegho asked, barely managing to move his lips.

Yeghsa lunged into the cart. She took Yegho's frozen hands into hers, kissed him, sobbed. She then bombarded him with questions, and in between her queries spoke breathlessly about a thousand things.

"Yegho, my darling," she kept saying, "live! Please live for the kids!"

It took him quite an effort to respond. "Woman," he said in a struggling voice, "Garbis was dying. Quick, find his mother, tell her to distribute bread to the poor for his salvation."

Yeghsa was about to say something when he made a frantic hand signal, urging her to leave. She took a couple of steps away from the cart, but came back.

"Yegho," she wondered, "you didn't ask about Vartug and Mariam."

"Are they alive?" he asked.

"What a question," she said indignantly. "I'd give my blood for their safety. Vartug can't wait to see you. She's been learning a new prayer every day, like you'd wanted her to."

That made him happy, bringing tears to his God-fearing eyes.

All of a sudden, a couple of men roughly pushed Yeghsa aside, spewing curses. They wanted her out of the way; the cart was full and ready to head out.

As the vehicle barreled toward the city center, Yeghsa breathlessly ran after it, in the pouring rain, desperate not to lose its track. There were many hospitals in Damascus. Which was Yegho being taken to?

By the time she reached the first major square, she had lost sight of the cart. Her head spun. Her clothes were soaked. She couldn't go on. She plonked herself down at the foot of a tramway pole, where she wept for a long time.

For the next several weeks, she took daily pilgrimages to this or that hospital. She grew used to being thrown out. Nevertheless she kept begging, entreating. Sometimes she chanced upon a more or less compassionate doctor or officer in charge who lied to her just to be rid of her. "Come back on Monday," they'd tell her. "That's our visitation day."

With renewed hope, she would excitedly wait for Monday. But when Monday arrived and she once again tried her luck, some guard would viciously kick her out. "Visitation's over," she'd be yelled at. "Don't come back till Friday."

Still, none of this could hold her back. She went on to witness quite a few iterations of the ongoing farce at hospital entrances. At best, some hospital clerk would feign to scan through his log, only to tell her there was no record of a patient named Yegho.

A month later, in church, she met an Armenian doctor. She could tell by his red collar that he was a physician. Once the Mass was over, she introduced herself, tearfully told him Yegho's story, and beseeched him to allow her a visit to her husband, even if it were for half an hour.

The good doctor jotted down Yegho's particulars on a crumpled piece of paper. He then asked her to go see him the following day at the hospital where he worked.

That Monday, the doctor went to a hospital which specialized in the treatment of typhus and dysentery cases. He carefully reviewed two weeks' worth of logs. Yegho's name didn't turn up. But the doctor persevered. He checked logs going back 20 days, a whole month.

At long last, he found what he was looking for. The admittance clerk's note that stared at him gave him pause and saddened him. Yegho had not made it alive to the hospital. He was listed in the "Deceased" column, with the designation "Dead on arrival."

For Menon

Nazeli was a hapless woman of about 40. With a slim figure of average height and an attractive face, she elicited in her interlocutor a mixture of solicitousness and affection, even at first sight. Every time she approached someone and began to speak, her cheeks reddened, and at once she lowered her eyes in hesitation and embarrassment.

In an odyssey that had begun in a faraway place, she had reached the Armenian refugee camp on the shore of the Suez Canal. Her birthplace was the breathtaking countryside which had beheld the snow-capped heights of Mount Argeus, in Kesaria, since time immemorial.

Many among Nazeli's family had perished during the massacres and deportations. Only a handful of her fellow townspeople as well as her 12-year-old daughter, Menon, remained alive.

Prior to Nazeli's arrival in the camp, she and her daughter lived two years in a poor Bedouin village somewhere in the Muwan Desert. Along with the other refugees who had ended up there, Nazeli was forced to convert to Islam.

She struggled in the harshest of circumstances, barely eking out a living. As she toiled away for mere survival, she also made certain to avoid drawing the attention of greedy and lascivious eyes, and, particularly, to keep her rose, the ravishing Menon, whose astounding beauty seemed to bloom all too quickly, hidden in the shadows.

Yet a diamond can grow even more enchanting, even more radiant, in the shadows. Surely this radiance is the strife of light against dark.

People talked. They gossiped about Nazeli. "All she's doing is fattening her chicken so she can sell it at a high price to some Arab rooster" was the gist of their jabs.

Virtually ostracized by her own compatriots and deeply offended, Nazeli often wept behind a mound, near the hillock where every day she and a group of refugees went to collect grass.

One day, the young son of a local sheikh came with great ceremony to Nazeli's hut, bearing many gifts. He formally asked Menon's hand in marriage. After all, weren't both he and Menon, by the grace of God, Muslims? He was rich and handsome, and perfectly able to add one more wife to his harem.

Nazeli was devastated. She called on the suitor as well as the imam, the village chief, and some elders in order to appeal to their sense of fairness. They all proved deaf to her tears and entreaties, her objection that Menon was simply too young to marry.

The wedding was enforced. Menon, ensconced in a dazzling litter on the back of a decorated camel, was triumphantly escorted off in a procession of horsemen, amid the women's cries of joy.

With an inconsolable grief in her heart, Nazeli returned to work the following morning. Now she was all alone, and life had to go on.

Months rolled by. Menon often sent letters to Nazeli, anxious to put her mind at ease. "Don't cry, mother," she wrote. "I am well. Don't forget me. Pray for me."

Pray was all Nazeli could do. At night, in her earthen hut, her eyes fixed on a piece of glimmering clay, she murmured, "Give me a ray of hope, Lord, a miracle."

That ray of hope did not take long to appear.

In late July 1918, a storm broke from the depths of the desert. Cannons blasted from afar, and, one fine day, before the sun reached its zenith, the women gathering grass watched in disbelief as columns of horsemen charged through the desert.

The news spread fast. It was the victorious British army, in hot pursuit of Turkish troops, who, with arms painted with the blood of the Armenian people, still raised them to the sky to plead for strength and success on the battlefield.

As much as they could, the victors at once fed and clothed the skeletal, famished human beings that were the Armenian refugees. Then they loaded them by the dozen onto their trucks and drove them away. As the vehicles darted into the sand, the refugees raptly gazed at the surrounding landscape, and particularly the grassy hillock which had been their Golgotha throughout their wretched existence in the village.

Where were they being taken to? No one could tell as yet. All the refugees knew was that, with the yearning for life once again sprouting in them, they were headed to a promised land, in the victorious footsteps of a Christian nation.

They went from one station to the next, at breakneck speed and with beating hearts. Once they reached Jerusalem, they were allowed to offer prayers in a cathedral. They all knelt down before a cross and lamented their dead.

Withdrawn into a corner of the church, Nazeli prayed at length for her delicate Menon, who now languished in slavery.

***

On a sunny September morning, along with hundreds of other refugees, Nazeli stepped foot on the refugee camp by the Suez.

Months after her first prayer in that Jerusalem church, she remained spellbound by the luminous visions which the temple had evoked. Indeed, she believed that after so much suffering and so many victims, omnipotent God, protector of the cross, would deem it appropriate to perform the miracle of freeing her daughter from captivity.

More months passed, but the miracle never materialized. Once every few weeks, fresh groups of refugees arrived in the camp, rekindling a sense of hope in the mournful hearts of the residents, energizing them once again. There were also rare instances in which a group of newcomers included long-lost friends, relatives, or family members. Such cases were marked by heartbreaking scenes of reunification, as loved ones tearfully embraced one another.

Every time a new group came ashore, Nazeli ran toward it breathlessly, hoping to reunite with her daughter. With eyes wide open, her hand on her chest, and pallid with emotion, she inspected one by one the faces of the hundreds of Armenian deportees stepping off the big ships.

Some screamed, others beamed with joy. Still others, hanging on to bundles of rags that were often twice their size, greedily and stubbornly refused to hand them over to the camp workers offering help. Their mistrust could hardly be blamed. They came from a land that was devastated by thieves, and every one of them had been robbed of the lives of many family members, their properties, and honor.

After intently and anxiously scanning the faces of the newcomers and murmuring, "That's no her... No, that's not her either," Nazeli would draw a deep sigh. As the last few deportees disembarked and were taken to their tents, she stood there petrified, leaning against the rail, gazing at the length of the canal, until the pier guard rudely ordered her to leave.

Yet despite an unrelenting string of disappointments, after years of witnessing bloodbaths and destruction, and enduring the constant delaying of the lone dawn she waited for, Nazeli never ceased to hope. She waited and hoped, shielded by an unshakeable faith.

Every time an official visited the refugee camp, Nazeli approached him, and, with downcast eyes and a red face, timidly told him of her pain: "I have a daughter. Her name is Menon…"

Everyone heard her story with great interest. They also jotted down, on the first piece of paper they could get their hands on or the back of a pack of cigarettes, Menon's particulars, including the man who had forcibly taken her as a wife, his line of work and place of residence, and so on. Invariably, these officials would go on to reassure Nazeli about the prospect of recovering her daughter. Weren't they, after all, respected members of the National Union, whose very mandate was to search for and rescue unfortunate Armenian girls and women scattered across the deserts of Arabia?

In the meantime, Nazeli went to the camp's thatched chapel on a daily basis, on the first toll of the bell. After making the sign of the cross three times as she went in, she genuflected at her favorite spot near the altar, and prayed.

***

Several, seemingly unending, months went by, until one day, with the arrival of a new wave of refugees, fresh news were delivered, about scores of Armenian women and girls who lived among nomadic Arabs in not only Gwara, Aqaba, and essentially everywhere in between, but Muwan as well.

The news about Menon was brought by an Armenian young man who had escaped from the Muwan.

A few of us interviewed him before he could talk to Nazeli. He said he had offered Menon to escape with him, but she had refused for the sake of her child, preferring to wait for another opportunity in the future. After hearing this, we asked the young man to not share it with Nazeli, so as to spare her further consternation.

Afterwards he told the teary-eyed Nazeli that Menon was well and looked forward to the blissful day when she would be able to safely leave the lair of her captors and reunite with her mother.

In the following weeks, Nazeli pleaded with various officials to find a way to rescue her daughter. They all listened patiently and were deeply moved, wrote down the relevant details, and heartened her.

Yet Nazeli was descending into a state akin to hopelessness — a sentiment that was unfamiliar to her world view and threatened to undo her very spirit.

***

This, too, was to pass.

One day, while praying in the chapel, Nazeli had an epiphany. She was ecstatic. She ran out, found some recent refugees who worked in the city, and asked them to buy some materials for her. For the next two weeks, she worked day and night on a crochet.

Once her project was completed, she placed her handiwork in a small bundle. On the first Sunday that followed, at dawn, she went to church in the city, more jubilant than she had ever been.

She piously and deferentially walked up to the senior priest and opened the bundle before him. It was a chalice veil, embroidered with tiny blue and red beads. Nazeli requested that the priest use the veil during Mass that day.

"It is for Menon, Reverend Father," she said.

As the Mass was performed, Nazeli's eyes, exuding a self-effacing rapture, were fixed on the colorful veil blanketing the chalice. In those moments of utter devotion, she believed that God would at last notice her predicament and take pity on her... that the miracle was about to transpire, emanating from that chalice and transforming her daughter's fate... that the end of the torment was very much close at hand...

The choir's dulcet voices and melancholic hymns filled the doleful hearts of the hundreds of congregants with a soaring sense of mysticism.

Once again, there rang the solemn refrain of the choir: "Give peace to our world and freedom to the slaves. Lord, have mercy..."

Through this earnest appeal to providence, Nazeli expected to be granted what she most desired, and believed to have come one step closer to experiencing the imminent freedom of her child.

Hand on chest, she wept sporadically, as her lips trembled with a fervent plea: "Lord, have mercy..."

The vanquished cross

With a big cane in his hand, a paltry bundle on his back, and his white beard sullied with a mixture of dust and sweat, he panted as he climbed up a road, under a scorching sun.

The poor man was worn out. He had walked for three days. He came from afar, from the Muwan Desert, had crossed the rocky heights of Solt in order to reach Jerusalem. He had spent the previous night crouched against a rock, somewhere near the Dead Sea, shivering.

He was about 60 years old. He had a slightly hunched back, a ruddy complexion, and a pair of deep-blue, martyr's eyes, in which it was not difficult to read the suffering that accompanies unspeakable horrors.

He was an Armenian priest. After wandering with his flock for three long months, having witnessed the deaths of thousands along the deportation route, in the waters of the Euphrates and the sands of Arabia, he had at last arrived in Der-Zor. He lived there with the only family from his village that had survived the massacres. Gone was his once-joyful flock. The men and boys were slaughtered by the Turks; girls and young women were abducted; and many of the remaining women were violated.

A year later, the priest had escaped to the Muwan Desert, along with two elderly. They had placed the last of their measly savings in the greedy hands of Bedouin for the privilege of being taken to Muwan, which they thought of as a promised land compared with Der-Zor.

They settled in Solt, joining several Armenian families which had begun taking baby steps to rebuild their lives. On his first day in Solt, the priest had cried tears of joy and entreated the Almighty to take pity on the Armenian survivors scattered throughout the Middle East. Soon afterwards, Solt's tiny Armenian community had helped him establish a makeshift chapel in a hut, and he had begun to perform his priestly duties for the refugees.

In the fall of 1916, the Turkish government's dark order of com-

pulsory Islamification reached Solt. Within a day, every single Armenian refugee converted to Islam.

The priest was horrified at the sight of this turn of events, which felt like a final insult dealt to his people's injuries. He now felt absolutely alone, and once again remembered the countless acts of barbarism he had witnessed since 1915, including the decimation of his hometown.

Near midnight, following hours of rumination, he wore a tattered abaya, covered his head with a keffiyeh, made a small bundle of provisions, took his cane, and, making the sign of the cross and murmuring blessings for his Islamized flock, left the village.

After walking for three days across an unfamiliar expanse, he edged closer to Jerusalem, where his anointed forehead would not have to kneel before the Turk's sill.

As he approached the Mount of Olives, he felt his heart fill with a divine bliss. He paused and gazed at the Holy City, with its golden crosses. He then knelt down, took out a large, iron cross which he had brought from his village church, and kissed it.

It was almost evening. With a brightened, tranquil spirit, he stood up and continued his trek. Suddenly vivacious as a child, he ran down stony pathways, toward Gethsemane. With great trepidation and breathlessly, he crossed the Valley of Josaphat, climbed up Mount Zion, slid like a shadow down the hill, and ran through the Old gate like an old prey being pursued by a dreadful foe. Finally, as he found himself in front of his people's gracious monastery, the Cathedral of Saint James, he stopped and made the sign of the cross.

He took off his grimy shoes and keffiyeh, and, after placing them, together with his cane and bundle, by the door of the church, went inside. In the half-darkness, guided by the faint lights of the lanterns, he proceeded feverishly toward the altar, before which he fell to his knees.

He was alone in the church. He wept a long time. Afterwards he spread his arms, and, in the profound silence of the cathedral, began to pray, as though chanting a tragic song. He begged the Almighty's forgiveness for blaspheming, for swearing at him on account of his utter indifference toward the destruction of the Armenian nation. He then beseeched the Lord to hasten to come to the aid of the Armenian people, whose sons and daughters now languished in the Arabian desert, dying of hunger and disease, or else forcibly being converted to Islam.

"Kindle hope in our hearts, Lord, bring us light!" he said.

All of a sudden, his frazzled arms fell to his sides.

He rested his forehead on the marble edge of the altar and closed his eyes. His head spun. He could hear a thousand and one voices rising from his depths. In his mind's eye, millions of stars, uprooted from the firmament, danced in the enormous darkness and tiny planets tumbled one after the other, at breakneck speed, while he seemed to be but an atom, an insignificant toy resembling a ball, which ceaselessly churned along with the heavenly bodies.

The priest remained in the throes of a sweet torpor for quite a while, with his eyes closed, carried away by that race of the imagination. It was something akin to a vision, a hallucinatory state which afforded him the illusion of the tangible possibility of the miracle he sought.

Some time later, a teenage boy dressed in black walked up to the priest. The church was about to close for the day. The boy seemed perplexed by the sight of the genuflecting peasant's luminous face. He asked him, with the sweetness of a caring grandson: "What's wrong, grandfather?"

"The miracle will happen, my child," the priest replied. "I had a vision: the unbelievers will be crushed; the cross will prevail. I strayed from my faith. I was lost, unhappy. Now I'm delivered."

With this he stood up, and asked the boy to take him to the primate.

Piously, with the reticence of a simple villager, and his hand placed against his chest, the priest entered the office of the archbishop, who was a ruddy-faced, portly fellow.

"Your Grace," the priest began, "I saw the atrocities with my own eyes. I witnessed the annihilation of our people and the trampling of its honor. I held death, touched it with my hands, yet survived…

"I come from Solt. The godless have proceeded to Islamize our people. And as though all this weren't enough, they now snatch away our virgins legally!"

"Well," the archbishop said, "what's done is done. We are powerless to do anything about it. At this time, compliance is our law and religion." Then he added, with a smirk, "Now tell me exactly why you've come here."

Struck by this bewildering reaction, the priest looked around helplessly. His eleventh-hour hopes for a miracle were suddenly fizzling out. He fell silent for a moment. Clearly not everyone shared his view of the catastrophe that had befallen his people.

"But, Your Grace, they were about to Islamize me too," he said with a gesture of desperation.

"It wouldn't matter, Father," the archbishop replied. "You have no choice but to accept Islam."

"Why do you think it wouldn't matter?" the horrified priest managed to say, and, with trembling hands, took a step forward.

"Let's cut to the chase," the archbishop said as he stood up. "You will spend the night here, get some sleep. You will leave at dawn, making sure not to be seen by anyone, and head straight back to your ancestral mountains. We are not allowed to harbor any Armenian fugitive here without the explicit permission of the Turkish authorities. A breach on our part would mean the ruination of this monastery. Go back, Father."

"Your Grace," the priest said, "I am going crazy. At least give me some hope."

"This is no time for hollow consolations," the archbishop concluded. "Just go back."

The priest was seething. Suddenly his lovely, martyr's eyes assumed a diabolical glint, his features strained, and his beard trembled. Like a madman, he hurled himself out of the office, ran down the stairs, and grabbed his bundle, keffiyeh, and cane. He then raised his arms, and, foaming at the mouth, screamed at the top of his lungs: "May you be damned, Turkish people! May grass not sprout on your soil! May your sun be extinguished forever! May the centuries tell of the tragedy you have brought to our hearths! May you be damned, bloody Crescent and vanquished Cross!"

Subsequently, consumed by a burgeoning, savage fury, he pulled out the jewel-laden cross from his chest and flung it violently to the ground. He went on to stomp and crush to pieces the noble relic of the black days… Then, like a deranged phantom, he pierced his cane into the night and darted off.

Hunchbacked Manuel

His face oozed such an imploring meekness that you would at once presume he was a child of misfortune.

He was about 13, with a hunchback and a pair of moist, light-gray, twinkling eyes which brimmed with sweetness and affection.

He came by our tents every day, with the hesitation and timidity of someone who has been abused. He stood a few feet away, next to a mangled, bare tree, and waited for hours on end, his eyes fixed on the tents.

The first day he appeared, our officers took great pity on the poor boy. The psychology of the Turkish officers was clear enough: since the young beggar had a hunchback and a large, deformed head, he looked like a strange "animal;" and the Turks, having lost all human feelings, had apparently compensated for this loss by developing in themselves a love of animals. Indeed, the only creatures toward which they demonstrated heartfelt compassion were those "without a tongue."

To the best of my recollection, our battalion was stationed for no more than ten days in a place past Kulek, near Darson [Tarsus]. We had set up camp across a burned-down glade, where only a handful of maimed trees remained standing.

Hunchbacked Manuel: this is how our men referred to the boy. The first two days he came by, the officers filled his tattered waist strap with bread and raisins. On the third day, the officers began to grumble. On the fourth day, they wanted to kick him out. After all, he was overdoing it, and there was a limit to their compassion.

It was at this point that I signaled to the disabled beggar boy to approach me.

He told me his father was a carpenter. He said his parents and grandmother had led a comfortable life before his father was conscripted into the army two years ago and consigned to hard labor. They hadn't heard from him since.

In order to survive, his mother did menial work, such as washing clothes, at neighbors' homes while he, for almost a year now, had taken to begging.

He told the story of their misfortunes, as well as the tragedies that had struck his hometown, with such restrained bitterness and chronological precision that I found myself astounded by his maturity.

He told me about the deportation of Armenian families a year ago, the humiliating circumstances under which they had sold their possessions to Turkish neighbors, and even the ridiculously low amounts that were given for their valuables. Since, at that time, families of Armenian soldiers were still afforded a modicum of respect by the Turkish populace, Manuel's family was spare being deported.

I rewarded Manuel handsomely but asked him to not come back, to not debase himself before the Turkish officers.

There were tears in his eyes. He shook his big head, kissed my hand, looked around as though to make sure no one threatened to confiscate the money I gave him, and went away in quick steps.

Three days later, I once again saw him next to his usual tree, slumped, dejected, almost become one with the trunk. His eyes conveyed a mixture of fear and shame.

"Manuel, why are you here again?" I asked, a bit sternly.

The seriousness of my tone froze him. He covered his head with his waist strap and began to sob.

"Don't be sad, son," I said, now with a softened, affectionate voice. "I guess you were forced to come back. Tell me what's bothering you."

"I pleaded with my mother; I told her I was ashamed and would rather walk to the end of the world than come to these tents," he explained. "But she wouldn't hear of it. She beat me. She said right now Turkish officers are the richest people around."

He couldn't look me in the eye. As he spoke with his head buried in his waist strap, fear was still very much evident in his trembling voice.

"So you're here to beg again," I said gently.

"No," he snapped. "I will not go to the Turks! Let me just tell you a fairy tale and you'll give me ten paras [Turkish money]."

"Very well," I said, surprised by the offer. "Go on then."

Suddenly he seemed overjoyed. He rubbed his hands together, stepped closer, with deference, bent down next to my chair, took out a filthy rag from his waist strap, and started to shine my shoes.

"Manuel," I said, "you don't have to do that. I just want to hear your

fairy tale, then you'll earn your money and be on your way."

This remark, too, offended his sensitive soul.

He put the rag back into his belt, and, gazing at me apprehensively, began his story.

"Once upon a time, there was a king, and he had a beautiful daughter…"

He went on to tell, in deeply felt, dazzling detail, the fairy tale of the king's daughter, which ended with forty days and nights of wedding celebrations.

"Well done!" I exclaimed. "You tell a good story. You earned your money. From now on, try to make an honorable living."

I gave him 40 paras, along with some bread — which, in those days, was in extremely short supply.

Afterwards, reflecting back, I was fascinated by the fervor with which this teenage boy told the story of the king's love-struck daughter.

Manuel was back the following day, fearful still but relatively self-confident. Once again, he could not bring himself to raise his eyes.

"I will tell you a new and beautiful fairy tale for ten paras," he said.

"Please do," I said absentmindedly. This form of begging was at least more creative. For ten paras, the Bedouin belt out lecherous songs and make their little girls perform a belly dance, whereas this Armenian boy, with his sensitive and colorful storytelling, had found an honorable way to earn his daily bread.

"Once upon a time, there were two brothers, one very brawny, the other thin. They crossed mountains, they crossed valleys, and came to a cave where there were 40 demons…"

Manuel told the story in little verses. It was a wonderful folk epic that took on a distinct beauty, even a measure of spiritual nobility, in his delivery.

For the next five days, Manuel returned at the same hour, a bit more encouraged every day. He came into my tent with an incrementally prouder, more self-confident demeanor. For five days, he told me marvelous fairy tales, all full of love, miracles, and heroic deeds.

The last day he appeared, we were busy dismantling our tents. He wept bitterly, leaning against the tree trunk.

"Why are you crying, Manuel?" I asked.

"You were kind," he said. "I felt big in your tent. Now I will die…"

52

"Oh, no. Don't say such things. A lot of tents will still come and pass through these mountains."

I took out 40 paras to give him. He hesitated.

"But I didn't tell you a fairy tale today," he said.

"All right," I said. "Tell me a new story."

"Once upon a time, there was a king…"

"I know that one."

He was taken aback. He placed his hand on his head, as though trying to extract something.

"Once upon a time, there were two brothers…"

"I know that one too," I said with a chuckle.

The poor boy was at a loss. Holding his head with both hands, he began to tell me, one by one, the stories of the previous days, only to be interrupted at the beginning of each.

"Manuel," I said, "it seems to me you've run out of stories."

There were tears in his eyes. Like a criminal caught red-handed, he said humbly, "I don't know any new ones. My grandmother didn't teach me any. Yesterday I begged her to tell me a fairy tale. But she was busy. Then she was tired and went to bed early."

"So it was your grandmother who taught you the fairy tales?"

"You looked like you enjoyed them, so I learned a new one every night and told it to you the morning after."

We both fell silent. My mood had changed. Staring into space, I contemplated life's cruelties.

"Don't be cross," Manuel said. "If you were to stay here, I would've learned two more stories for tomorrow. If you like, I'll tell you the story of our neighbor's lost bride…"

"Go on," I said mechanically, gazing at his despondent face.

"The Turks just tore down our neighbor's house. It used to be a big house, three stories high. My mother always went over for work. They had a beautiful bride, with eyes black as raisins. I tell you, there was fire in those eyes. Her hair was so long that sometimes I dreamt that it was wrapped around my neck… She used to give me so many things!

"All of them — father, mother, child — are now gone. My grandmother told me about them and we all cried. Five days ago, a farmer brought a letter to Doctor Christy. It was sent by the beautiful bride. She wrote that she was in a faraway place and had become the wife of a colonel. She asked for help. That night, in front of the picture of the Virgin

Mary, my grandmother and I said the Lord's Prayer for the bride of our neighbor. She was so very beautiful... May God gladden her heart... May the angels wipe her tears."

Once again, I was amazed by Manuel's passionate style. I put five coins in his hand.

"Manuel," I said, "I wish that tonight you and your grandmother would light the lantern again in front of the Virgin Mary's picture. This time pray for me, son. Don't forget. Pray from your heart for the lost ones of an unfortunate traveler."

1918

The ravine nest

Judging by his features, he must've been about 20 years old. He had a flaxen mustache whose sparse strains barely shaded his life-breathing, full lips. His light-chestnut, bluish eyes were given to an always delightful, somewhat haughty, smile, which could hardly veil the innocent vanity of an extremely handsome and dapper young man.

He already had a gleaming epaulette on his shoulder, and, true to form, comported himself as an army officer full of hope and glittering dreams for the future.

He was not what you might call a deep thinker. Rather, he personified the type that loves life for its own sake and deems the world a traitor the minute the latest love affair comes to an end.

Though not a full-fledged egotist, he had an artless philosophy of appreciating life's light and easy pleasures, which made him see the suffering and laughter of the world through a strictly personal prism. This was in no small measure due to the fact that he was his mother's only son, long in the habit of analyzing everything purely within the context of his own emotions.

His mother, Mrs. Sevian, worshipped him. She beamed with joy every time her lovely son came home. He was now a grown man, resplendent in his officer's uniform, with a sword dangling on his side, a shiny collar gracing his neck, and a silver baton in his hand.

He was the Little Hagop of yesteryears, the family's chirping Blondo. This was what his mother called him, even after he had reached adolescence, on account of his golden locks.

Having lost her husband while still quite young, Mrs. Sevian was left all alone in the world, save for her beloved firstborn as well as young daughter, Ashkhen. Ever since becoming a widow, she had concentrated the adulation of her heart on her son, perhaps vicariously living through him the joys that were denied her in her youth.

Indeed, so blind and absolute was her dedication to him that if ever it were to be pointed out to her that she was spoiling him to an absurd, almost pathological degree, I am certain she would be shocked and devastated by the suggestion.

Influenced by the example of their town's notables, Mrs. Sevian had sent Hagop to a Turkish school, which he began to attend when he was eight years old.

The family was well-to-do. As Hagop grew into manhood, his mother continued to do everything possible to ensure his happiness. His slightest wish was sacrosanct; and whenever one of his impossible whims remained unfulfilled, it seemed as though a grievous pall bore down the household, for several days at a time.

Therefore it must be considered something of a miracle that such unconditional and unbridled devotion on the part of Mrs. Sevian did not end up making a rascal out of her son. Quite the contrary: Hagop excelled at school, always striving to be at the top of his class; and although he constantly obsessed over dressing well, looking good, and attracting girls, not to mention shining brightly among his Turkish classmates, his youthful vanity was more than matched by his kindness and keen sense of moral conduct.

While still in high school, Hagop added to his name the epithet Hilmi [meaning mild-mannered], which was in vogue in those days. Subsequently he was known by his school chums as Aghob Hilmi.

Hagop entered the military school of Istanbul at a time when we Armenians had joined the Turks in freely singing the song of brotherhood and equality.

At the outset of the mobilization in 1914 and prior to joining his battalion, Hagop, who had just become an officer, traveled to his hometown, in order to kiss his mother's hand and impress everyone with his military finery.

The following morning, a tearful Mrs. Sevian bid her son farewell, along with neighbors and friends who had gathered in front of their home.

"Blondo, don't forget me and your kid sister," she said. "You're carrying our lives with you."

***

Flood waters had formed a track which started at the foot of the Achi Baba, a height that dominates the Gallipoli Peninsula, and zigzagged its way down to Domuz Dere, toward the sea. At one point, where the waters had transformed the landscape into a ravine, a terrible mass of boulders jutted out. Stooped into a curve and extending its wings out above the abyss, the mass enclosed on its side a cavern that was reminiscent of an impregnable eagle nest. Now it was the "home" of a doctor, an old friend, who served in a small artillery unit installed in the canyon below.

The boulders' jarring shape, frightening dimensions, and vertiginous position made it a sight to behold, strangely beautiful and poetic. More importantly, the cavern it enclosed made for an ideal shelter against bombardments.

We referred to the cavern as the ravine nest. Sometimes, in his spare time inside it, my doctor friend wrote letters to me. They reached me at our hell on Earth, the far side of Sed-ul-Bahr — where I served with an infantry battalion, on the first line of fire.

Often, toward evening, when the fighting somewhat subsided, I made an excuse to take a break, and, lowering my head to my waist, ran across the trenches, in order to dodge the inevitable volley of sniper fire, and headed to the ravine nest.

The doctor and I hugged every time I went over. After all, these gatherings of ours were tantamount to resurrections, considering that I was still able now and then to take a respite from the hails of bombs and bullets to spend some time with my pal, with a glint of hope in my eyes and the will to life still in my chest.

"Let others rush off to the other side; I have no intention of dying," I used to say.

Also to join us at the ravine nest was Blondo, Mrs. Sevian's son.

Gone were the disdainful sparkle of his eyes, his glittering pretty-boy dreams. Despite his officer's rank, he had been taken off the frontline and assigned to a transport battalion, where he served in a demeaning position, as a deliverer of troop provisions.

The sadness which enveloped Hagop's face elicited a feeling of brotherly sympathy. He was our junior and we loved him dearly. Long used to the pleasures of a cloudless life, he now struggled in the grip of a boundless suffering. Sometimes he found it all too much and broke down in front of us, but, invariable, my doctor friend's dry sarcasm brought him around.

Often the three of us watched the dusk unfold, when the setting sun made the sea look like a field of fire before vanishing behind Imros Island.

We were enamored of those twilights. As we watched the blazing sea, from the side of the boulders, we took turns to give wings to our dreams and hopes, yearned for the liberation of our martyred nation, embraced the consoling images of justice and vengeance.

"Just one letter: that's all I got from Bozanti," Hagop once said. "It's been two months. I wonder what happened to my mother and sister."

"God will help," I said, for the sake of saying something, fully aware that no words could ease his pain.

"God will help all right," my doctor friend echoed mockingly.

It was the ravine nest that transformed Blondo. The bloody sunsets of Domuz Dere enchanted him, spilling into his soul a red hue, an epiphany, which was never to leave him. He was now focused entirely on the fate of his family. He knew that those lofty pronouncements of justice and brotherhood ruminated from behind the desks of Turkish luminaries were but the cogs of a grand sham; and, more than anything else, it killed him to think of the dangers that must've faced his rosy-cheeked, dark-eyed, dazzling sister, whom he worshipped.

"I'm choking," he used to say. "There's something like a nightmare rising in me. Help me, my friends, give me hope!"

"We were as helpless," I told him once, "and had no choice but to surrender our loved ones to the deserts. But don't give up, Blondo. Preserve your energies. The time will come for you to lunge at the sons of the crime."

***

On December 28, 1915, a chilly, bright day, we left the ravine nest. The previous night, the Allied armies had withdrawn. We were crestfallen.

Pretending to be busy elsewhere, we kept to ourselves for several hours so as to avoid having to take part in the jubilation of the Turkish battalions. What cheap euphoria! If only it were an actual victory.

Sunk into the dolor of someone being led to the guillotine, we said goodbye to our lair, trudged down the mountain, and, against the deafening cheers of the Turkish troops, secretly mourned the death of our hopes. It appeared that the Great Crime would be left unpunished; the salvation of our people would be delayed once more; the waiting would last long, very long, like death itself.

After replenishing our decimated military division in Istanbul, we began a long, arduous march toward Aleppo.

When we reached Keller, I once again ran into Blondo. I could barely recognize him. He had lost quite a bit of weight and was frighteningly pallid.

That night, after setting up camp on a hillside, Blondo and I took a stroll. As we walked toward the canyon below, we noticed a handful of gray tents in the distance, hidden amid heaps of stones.

"Let's go there," Blondo said. "Let's see if anyone knows anything. Back in Islahiye and Tahta Kopru, I saw some tents scattered in the fields. I went from one to the next. The people inside were all Armenian women and kids. Some train-station chief or military officer had held them there, God knows for what filthy purpose. I asked the deportees all sorts of questions. They weren't from our part of the country. Nobody knew of my poor mother and sister."

We walked some more until we reached the tents. They were occupied by rail workers as well as elderly army laborers, mostly Armenians. They had escaped the brutal conditions of the army, especially since they knew they were marked to be massacred eventually.

Blondo proceeded to shoot questions.

"I have no idea, little brother," replied a scrawny old man. "Thousands passed by… Thousands of young women who had been uprooted… They were all shriveled, looked like phantoms… with tattered clothes, legs naked… It was as if they didn't give a damn anymore…I didn't see anyone from your town."

Blondo wouldn't give up. He kept inquiring, tent after tent. To no avail.

In the ensuing weeks, as we marched through the vast expanses of Anatolia, Blondo continued to ask around about his family. He loved his mother very much, but it was his young sister that had become the stabbing nightmare of his heart. What had become of the defenseless girl? Had the blooming rose of her cheeks withered? Had it been plucked?

The thought was unbearable to him. He felt the pressure of a tearing hand in his skull. Often he stopped and sat down by the roadside to ease the spinning of his head.

By the time we arrived in Aleppo, Blondo had fallen ill. Some Turkish officers from his battalion took him to a hospital. "Poor boy; apparently he's suffering," one of them said perfunctorily, as though showing token compassion for a dying animal on the roadside.

Blondo bolted out of the hospital on his tenth day.

"I was dying in there," he said when we were reunited in a tiny hotel room.

For the next five days, that hotel room became a converging point for the wingless falcons of the ravine nest. My doctor friend was now utterly silent, lost in grief. His entire family had been slaughtered by the Turks. Blondo fared as badly, since his relentless search throughout Aleppo had not turned up a single soul from his hometown. As for me, there was quite a bit on my plate too, yet I was also happy for having found my father, at the home of an Arab family.

On the sixth day, Blondo got word that survivors from his hometown were taken to Maskanah.

He had to act fast. His battalion was bound for the Caucasian frontline. With great difficulty, he obtained a ten-day leave of absence. That very evening, he hopped aboard a carriage and disappeared into the darkness.

***

The following day, as the carriage was passing through Tel Hafir, Blondo saw scatterings of cadavers along the road — they were the bodies of Armenians, left unburied, with the mouths covered with foam. He also saw half-dead wraiths — no longer looking quite human, with blank, sunken, inanimate eyes and swollen pupils, resembling frozen glass, and skin as wan as dried-out grass. They were the famished Armenian survivors of the deportations and massacres, destined to become tomorrow's corpses.

Blondo could no longer bear to look. He lowered his eyes as he gave handfuls of food to the wretched phantoms. He also paid the carriage driver a handsome bonus for waiting till nighttime to resume the journey. Thus Blondo would be spared the sight of the cadavers. And if robbers were to attack the carriage and kill him, so be it, he thought.

That night, in the carriage barreled across the countryside, Blondo was tormented by one lucid nightmare after the other. They were all about Ashkhen. Now and then, desperately trying to ward them off, he angrily wiped off his tears and stuck his head out of the window, by way of re-establishing contact with reality. Nothing had ever opened in his mind a wound so bloody as the image of the gentle, terror-stricken eyes of his sister in the face of a pack of lecherous monsters closing in on her. If only he were to be granted by providence the joy of finding her alive and kissing her sacred forehead, he would gladly give up anything, be stronger than ever to vanquish any conceivable difficulty.

The next morning, after crossing a serpentine trail through a string of knolls, they stopped at a bare foothill in order to give the horses some rest. Blondo walked to the edge of the hill, which had the appearance of a neck protruding into infinity. On his left, the Euphrates flew into the valley below, and, forming a half-circle, continued on into the desert. Also on his left, Blondo saw blue mountains in the far distance, opposite the Tigris. They must've been the mountains of Armenia. And on his right lay the dismal Maskanah Valley, stretching into the desert.

Suddenly he remembered his school desk, behind which he had devoured Turkish poetry with a feverish faith. He recalled the names of a number of authors who had written odes to this very valley. He began to recite a piece by Mualim Naji.

But he stopped after a line or two, feeling as though he had committed a sacrilege. After all, he realized quickly enough, the land stretching before him was one of the mass graves of his people. The Turk, having glutted himself on the pillage and slaughter of the Armenian population, had sent a portion of the remnants here, to this godforsaken land, where they, too, would be finished off in due course.

Blondo came down the hill, seething with rage.

There were no signs of human habitation except for the skeleton of a caravanserai in the distance, on the shore of the Euphrates. So this was Maskanah, where no less than 100,000 Armenians were either butchered or died of hunger or disease.

He also noticed a cluster of tents along the river shore.

His heart was pounding. He had a premonition that this valley was about to convey a message to him. A dreadful breath, like the ghost of a calamitous event, hovered above the landscape.

He advanced nervously toward the tents. As he drew close, literally thousands of human shadows began to materialize, running toward him. They were Armenian children and women, in rags, cadaverous and pallid beyond imagination, with fiendishly hollow, supplicating eyes. Blondo gave many of them whatever he had in his pockets and bag, without a second thought.

Eventually he lowered his eyes, and, becoming deaf to the heart-wrenching pleas of the kids surrounding him, walked on.

As he approached a dike, a new group of wraiths welcomed him. They were elderly Armenian women, gaunt, drained of life, and clearly famished, who stared at him in utter terror. He was an officer, a hyena, a Turk, who in all probability was out for a fresh bout of savagery.

"Mothers, do you know anyone from the town of T?" he asked in a trembling voice.

"He's Armenian! He's Armenian!" the women screamed ecstatically.

Blondo repeated the question.

"*I'm* from that town!" shouted a wretched woman in filthy, tattered clothes.

Blondo suddenly turned around, trembling.

She was an old woman with white hair, hollow cheeks, and an elongated chin. But her eyes, her big, beautiful eyes, were of his mother.

She recognized her long-lost child. Unable to speak a word, she rushed to him.

They cried bitterly in each other's arms. The other women wiped their tears, made the sign of the cross, and left the reunited mother and son alone.

It was close to evening. Sitting on the ground, by the bank of the Euphrates, Mrs. Sevian and Blondo gazed at one another in silence. Sometimes the poor woman was shaken by a spasm radiating through her entire body, like someone being subjected to an electric shock, and once again held her son's face in disbelief.

"Life has been too cruel, Blondo," she said. "Death did not come soon enough to save me."

Mrs. Sevian fell silent again, her eyes now fixed on the river. Blondo had a sneaking feeling that something catastrophic had transpired. He sensed that he was about to hear of it, and knew it would kill him. He tightened his heart, by way of preparing himself for the worst.

Just then, an old woman, a neighbor from their hometown, walked up to them. News of Blondo's arrival had already spread among the deportees.

"Don't be sad, son," she said. "Console yourself that your sister died with honor."

Blondo let out a faint cry. He then covered his face with his hands and broke into a sob.

Moments later, his skeletal mother straightened up, and, with a noble glint in her otherwise lifeless eyes, began to tell him Ashkhen's story.

"Listen, son," she said, "she was not dishonored. She died as immaculate as a lily.

"I gave away all my wealth, I counted away gold coins, to bring her safe and sound to this hell. I spent my last ten liras, and we were forced to eat grass, but couldn't save her from the hungry dogs of this place. One day, it was a gendarme. Another day, an official. And another, an Arab. They all harassed my innocent baby, wanted to take her as a wife. There was someone peering inside the tent every day. They hounded us. She spent the nights crying, praying desperately to be spared what awaited her. One morning, we found her body in a thicket by the water."

The sun was setting. As Mrs. Sevian and her son remained sitting on the sand, in the evening stillness, his grief was slowly but irrevocably being transformed into an emotion he had begun to harbor since his days at the ravine nest.

All of a sudden Blondo stood up.

The melancholy luster of his eyes was now replaced by a ferocious intensity. No longer was he the sobbing, meek boy of the previous moments.

"Sister," he shouted, pointing his outstretched hands at the Euphrates, "everything has died, but our honor is intact. From now on, may I be unworthy of my days if my hands are not painted with the foul blood of the savages. Come to me, come, day of reckoning…"

Having said his peace, Blondo helped his mother get up and gently held her by the arm. They vanished into the desert, within the last rays of sundown.

On an autumn day in 1916, a Turkish officer returning from the Caucasus told me that an Armenian sergeant by the name of Aghob Hilmi had escaped from their transport battalion to join the enemy side. The incident had prompted the Turkish army to decommission every single Armenian serviceman, irrespective of rank.

Soon afterward, I got word that Blondo had joined the Armenian fedayeen. He had, indeed, heeded the call of the ravine nest.

1918

Eaglet

"Any news from Ara? Did you get a letter, mom?" breathlessly asked a young woman dressed in a Turkish farajeh as she burst into Mrs. Medzarian's room. "Quick, tell me, mom, have you heard anything from Eaglet?"

"It's not what we expected, sweetheart," Mrs. Medzarian said. "I received a letter all right, but it's not from Eaglet. What I got is an extremely offensive reply from a Turkish businessman who had borrowed money from my husband. After reminding him of the large amount he owed us, I begged him to send us an insignificant amount, just to help us get by. He has refused."

Dejected, Shadan broke into tears.

"No, darling, please don't cry," Mrs. Medzarian said. "My heart is full of pain. Don't add fuel to the fire."

It was the usual tempest that once again exploded in the room of Mrs. Medzarian — recently given the Muslim name Leman Hanum — to be followed by a heavy, oppressive atmosphere.

The two women failed to find the words to console one another. They sat there for several minutes, shedding tears for Ara, the young man known to everyone as Eaglet. They hadn't heard from him in many long months.

Ever since childhood, Ara had been his mother's favorite, as much for his scintillating eyes as his rebellious and zestful character.

Behind their town, atop a cluster of steep boulders, there was a nest of black eagles which gazed at the village and the horizons beyond it.

When Ara was a little boy, Mrs. Medzarian liked to go out to their garden right before sundown, clasping him to her bosom. Standing under the willow tree, she cheerfully showed Ara the crest of the boulders in the distance, where groups of intrepid eaglets flapped their wings in their fledgling attempts to take to the sky.

Inspired by the sight of the fidgety baby eagles, Mrs. Medzarian jiggled Ara from side to side, and up and down, flung him up into the air, as though propelling him to fly, and caught him back as they both let out cries of joy. Reveling in her child's sparkling eyes and restless movements, Mrs. Medzarian held him tight to her chest and kissed him. "And you're my own eaglet," she used to say to him. "Tomorrow you, too, will flap your wings, you'll fly and be happy…"

Soon Ara's father, sisters, brothers, and grandmother often called him Eaglet.

***

Now Ara, Mrs. Medzarian's youngest son, had become a veritable eagle, even though his loved ones continued to call him their fiery Eaglet. He fought valiantly on the battlefield, as an officer in the Turkish army.

An unrelenting series of tragedies had struck the family since Ara had gone to fight on the frontlines. At the very start of the general deportation of Turkey's Armenian communities, the Turkish police had arrested Mrs. Medzarian's husband and two older sons and summarily hanged them, along with 40 other Armenian men — thus sparing them the fate of dying hungry and naked on a deportation road or being massacred in a remote ravine. A year later, Mrs. Medzarian was informed that both her married daughters had been abducted while being marched off to the east and their husbands were slaughtered in a gorge not far from their village.

Thanks to Ara's many pleas through official channels, his surviving loved ones, including his mother, grandmother, and youngest sister, Satenig, were granted exemption from being deported, as members of a serviceman's family.

After the town was stripped of its native Armenian community, the Turks took down the cross from the cupola of the church. They desecrated the paintings of saints and holy relics by throwing them into piles of excrement at the village square. Then they hung the paintings from the tails of mules and dragged them around, from one street to the next, laughing and swearing.

The centuries-old church was promptly turned into a mosque.

The few Armenian families that still remained in the village were forced to convert to Islam and assume Muslim names.

Several Armenian girls and young women were snatched away by Turkish men and now languished in various harems. Among them was

Shadan, formerly known as Arshaluys. A woman of dazzling beauty, she came from a rich family and for years was in love with Mrs. Medzarian's youngest son.

Yet Arshaluys and Ara had been unable to get married, due to the fierce and stubborn objections of the girl's father.

"Medzarian's son is nothing but a long-haired, Istanbul-educated, vogue-chasing fool," Arshaluys' father used to say. "I'll die before I give up my only daughter and wealth."

Despite the entreaties of Arshaluys and her mother alike, he had remained stone-hearted. In the meantime, the attachment between the two young lovers had grown ever stronger.

During the latter part of their town's deportations, when hundreds of Armenian families, carrying little bundles on their shoulders, were being driven off their ancestral hearths, a well-connected young Turk forced Arshaluys to marry him. He was the local veterinarian and enjoyed the unalloyed blessing of the town's Muslim elders in his pursuit of her.

"Arshaluys, my daughter, forgive me," her father told her as she was being escorted away. "I was so very cruel to you. I broke your heart and caused you much suffering. Please forgive me, my child."

Afterwards he was seen sitting on the ground, hitting his head to a wall and slapping himself like a madman.

Since becoming the veterinarian's wife, Arshaluys, who was renamed Shadan, often spent her days alone at home, with their housemaid, as her husband was gone for days at a time to make his rounds in nearby villages.

Yet having convinced her husband that Mrs. Medzarian, now Leman Hanum, was a close relative, Arshaluys had permission to visit her as frequently as she liked. The veterinarian had agreed to this only too gladly, both to please his wife, whom he adored, and, particularly, given that Leman Hanum's family consisted of two harmless women and a little girl, with not a trace of a male, adult or otherwise.

A year had passed since the start of the deportations and massacres.

Whenever her husband was away on business, Arshaluys visited her "aunt," on a daily basis, hankering for a bit of news from her lost love. These visits would invariably be colored with disappointment for Arshaluys. There would be nothing left to do for the two women except relive their pain through one another, renew their hope for Ara's miraculous reappearance, and hatch plans as though the miracle were close at hand.

67

Then, one day, the miracle did seem to be within reach. After months of waiting, they received a letter from Ara.

"Mother," he wrote, "I was gravely wounded in the Dardanelles. For a long time, as I swayed between life and death, I was unable to write you.

"But I didn't die. I knew you had prayed for me. Considering my injuries, the army has given me an indefinite discharge. I will be coming home soon — not on vacation, but to spend the rest of my days with you."

Mrs. Medzarian, her mother, and Arshaluys were overjoyed. Yet no sooner had they finished reading the letter that a dark suspicion crept in.

"This is not his handwriting," Mrs. Medzarian said. "Can it be that his friends are fooling me?"

"Your pain won't let you see straight anymore," her mother objected. "You see everything in black. Think about good things and God will give them to you."

"Well, probably he's too weak to write," Arshaluys put in. "Maybe he's had to ask a friend to do it for him. But it's Ara in those lines. There's no mistaking it. Can't be anyone else."

They discussed the matter at length until they convinced themselves that the letter was indeed from Ara, even though Mrs. Medzarian expressed one more reservation. "What about that talk about spending the rest of his days here? Why would he be discharged indefinitely?"

"Oh, come on, mother," Arshaluys countered. "The army is just rewarding him for his bravery, giving him as much time as he needs to recuperate at home."

Her words had a soothing effect, to the point that they allowed themselves to reminisce about good times.

"Mother," Satenig said, jumping up and down, "we'll go to the Icy Spring to welcome Ara. You're not going to tell him that my name has been changed to Sultan. He's going to lift me up and pinch my cheeks. He's going to kiss me. You won't tell him about my name, will you?"

"No, I won't, honey," Mrs. Medzarian reassured her. "There's a lot we shouldn't tell him."

At this, she and Arshaluys instinctively glanced at one other. The young woman was making a supreme effort to bite her tongue.

Mrs. Medzarian felt a shiver down her spine. For a moment forgetting her own woes, she put herself in Arshaluys' shoes. She remembered the days when Ara begged her to find a way so he and Arshaluys could wed, and admired the girl's stubborn, unconditional love. And now Mrs.

Medzarian's wounded son was about to return home, only to drink from the cup of misfortune. His two brothers had been murdered; his older sisters had vanished; and the love of his life now forcibly shared the bed of a Turk.

"No, mother, don't worry about me," Arshaluys said, as if reading Mrs. Medzarian's mind. "I've given up on any prospect of happiness. Let's think about Ara. Promise you won't tell him I'm the wife of a Turk. Please spare him that sorrow. I'll keep coming here as often as possible. I'll tell him I'm living with my mother. I'll say my father has been exiled and we should plan to elope… You will convince him to whisk me away. He had better save me from this predicament."

Mrs. Medzarian turned to Satenig. "Be careful, sweetheart," she said. "Don't you tell Eaglet that Arshaluys is now called Shadan, that she's the wife of a Turk."

***

In a glorious morning in April 1916, Mrs. Medzarian, her mother, Arshaluys, and Satenig walked to the Icy Spring, which was located on the main road, just outside the village.

The previous day, they had received a telegram from Ara informing them that he had reached a nearby city and would arrive home shortly. Their joy was tempered by their constant awareness of the tragedies they had sustained in his absence, tragedies which they had kept from him. But what were they to tell him if he asked about his absent brothers and sisters? And what would they do if he asked Arshaluys to marry him at long last?

They sat down under the shade of a willow tree next to the spring. After having spent a year among grieving women, Satenig frolicked to her heart's content, hopping around across the wide meadow.

A Turkish beggar approached them and asked for a handout in the name of God.

"Now which God would that be?" Mrs. Medzarian's mother shot back, fiercely staring at the poor man.

Mrs. Medzarian found her reaction imprudent, gave the beggar some money, and sent him on his way.

There was a steady stream of passersby. The women asked those heading to the village about the traveler they expected: "Did you come by a carriage? Did you notice a handsome officer inside it? He's been injured in battle…"

At around noon, a carriage appeared on the horizon. Hearts pounding, the women watched it advance toward them.

It was now barely a hundred steps away. They anticipated seeing Eaglet's captivating, fiery eyes through the small window of the carriage, and his powerful, nimble figure step down from the vehicle.

They saw neither.

As the carriage reached them, Mrs. Medzarian signaled the driver to stop. She then shyly walked up to the window and asked, "Kind travelers, did you, by any chance, come across an injured officer returning from the Dardanelles?"

"Mother, I'm here," said Ara's vigorous voice from the depth of the carriage.

All at once, the women screamed in jubilation and rushed to the door.

While Satenig lunged at the side step of the tall carriage, impatient to greet her brother, a sergeant who accompanied him helped him come down.

Mrs. Medzarian and her mother threw their arms around Ara, flooding his cheeks and neck with tears and kisses. Satenig, glued to her adored brother, rubber her cheeks against his side like a kitten and kept kissing his hand.

Only Arshaluys was left out. Forlorn, forgotten, she cried bitterly as she watched the reunion. She stood mere steps away from her lover, yet his lips remained cruelly closed to her pain-stricken face. If he no longer loved her, should not at least a tiny sentiment of pity have moved this indifferent, stone-hearted young man, for whom she had suffered, yearned, and prayed all those years? Indeed, she had adulated him to such a degree that he had become something of a divine figure in her life, her lone hope for salvation — and perhaps even happiness.

Noticing that Arshaluys remained standing at a distance, and assuming that anyone who did not partake in such an emotional reunion could not possibly be a close family member, the Turkish sergeant discreetly approached her and asked, "Hanum, are you a relative of the officer?"

"He's nothing to me!" Arshaluys snarled.

"Very well," the sergeant went on. "In fact, I was looking for someone not too close to him so I could reveal the truth. You see, Hanum, some four or five months ago, after a bomb exploded close by, my officer lost the light of his eyes. Now he's completely blind."

Arshaluys felt as though her head was struck by a colossal bludgeon. She felt the ground and the world itself caving in beneath her feet, the trees spinning around her, and, with her hopes lost forever, the entire cosmos fading away.

She let out a heart-rending cry. She turned pale and was about to collapse when the sergeant quickly held her, then gently helped her sit on the ground.

Suddenly realizing that Arshaluys was not among them, Mrs. Medzarian turned around and ran to her. "We were caught up in the moment and forgot about you, my child," she said apologetically.

She knelt before Arshaluys and hugged and kissed her, whispering words of relief. She then called out to Ara: "Eaglet, fly over here, son, it's Arshaluys. What are you waiting for?"

"Arshaluys?" Ara managed to mutter, and, fumbling his way through with his cane, scrambled in the direction of his mother's voice.

In his haste, he bumped into his grandmother.

Mrs. Medzarian, who at first had not thought anything of the large, black eyeglasses which enclosed her son's eyes, was now struck by a blood-curdling realization.

"Son, don't you see me?" she asked.

"I do, mother… I just need to wear these glasses for a while… But I do see all of you and I'm very happy."

Making a heroic effort, Arshaluys got up and affectionately gripped the young man's hand."

"Ara, do you see me?" she asked. "Quick, tell me, do you see me?"

"Of course I do, darling," he said. "I hear your voice. I feel as if my most cherished dreams are coming back to life at this moment."

"Ara, say it again, tell me, scream, reassure me that you still have your eagle's eyesight!"

"I never stopped seeing you, sweetheart, even in darkness," he persisted. "And now I see your beautiful face and the two large teardrops at the corners of your eyelids."

Arshaluys mechanically took her hands to her eyes.

Instead of the two teardrops she sought, a flood of tears streamed down her face. At that instant, unable to utter an other word, she flung her head at Ara's chest and sobbed, in an outpouring of love, compassion, and despair.

As the steady, ominous squawks of the crows filled the air, passersby curiously glanced at a group of three women and a little girl, who, crowded around a young army officer, cried their hearts out.

***

Anyone familiar with the mournful mood that once dominated the Medzarian household would be amazed by the serene hours of apparent bliss that now marked the family's life. Ara had been informed that their town's surviving Armenians, including his loved ones, had had no other choice but to convert to Islam.

Taking advantage of her husband's long absences, Arshaluys visited her "aunt" almost every day. Ara, on his part, waited impatiently for the moment Arshaluys would cheerfully enter their small house.

His mother, grandmother, and sister took great pains to keep from him the fact that Arshaluys was the wife of a Turk. Moreover, and in keeping with a decision they had taken prior to his arrival, they made a concerted effort to comport themselves as though they were in good spirits.

Ara never complained about his lot. Rather, he spent his days in reverie. He could surmount anything as long as he heard Arshaluys' enchanting voice, which filled his soul with an incalculable delight.

"My Eaglet, don't you get bored?" his mother would ask.

"No, mother, I've never been happier," he kept reassuring her.

Whenever Arshaluys visited, she led Ara to the garden. They sat next to the washtub, beneath the shade of the willow tree, sometimes holding hands, and chatted for hours, revisiting the past, rejoicing in each other's presence.

Toward evening, Arshaluys would get up, kiss Ara's forehead, and hasten to leave. "My mother is waiting," she'd say. "I'll be back tomorrow."

Often, at such moments, they embraced tenderly. Mrs. Medzarian would watch them from inside the house, acutely aware of their doomed love.

The nights were unbearable for Ara. Frequently he found it impossible to fall asleep, and, tired equally of his suffering and the permanent darkness that surrounded him, he buried his head in his hands and squeezed it until he broke into tears and began to pray, begging the Almighty for a sliver of light.

Being a believer, the very sincerity of his prayers gave him the strength to once again hope and allow himself a sense of well-being, with the image of Arshaluys' luminous face dominating his mind's canvas.

Yet something kept perturbing him. Back in the day, when he was healthy and handsome, when his eye sockets held not today's mangled pieces of flesh but a pair of eyes burning with passion, when he was a true eaglet, full of flight and song, Arshaluys was no less devoted than she was today. "Don't be sad, my beloved," she used to say, "my father's tyranny is nothing. If all else fails, we'll elope and hop from mountain to mountain."

Those words, which acquired the nobility of a Delphic oracle on her lips, now remained unspoken, had been so ever since his return.

Ara knew that Arshaluys' father had been murdered by the Turks. But he was told that her mother, who had always championed her daughter's union with him, was still alive. Why, then, didn't she ever come visit him? "I guess I'm no longer perceived as a suitable husband," he would conclude. "I'm a cripple, a dead-end. And it would be a crime to sacrifice a young woman's life and future by hitching her to someone like me. If Arshaluys has not left me yet, it's because she's an angel lulled by our sweet memories. An angel who feels compassion as strongly as she loves."

Almost every day, their conversations culminated in the big question mark about the future, as Ara needed to cling to a modicum of certainty. Instead all Arshaluys could do was shut his quivering lips with a kiss. "Let's live for today," she would say, "and not worry about the future."

***

Arshaluys' husband, who had fallen ill during a business trip, unexpectedly came home to recuperate. Naturally she was not allowed to leave his side.

Days of despondency ensued for Ara.

His mother told him Arshaluys was unwell and would be bedridden for a few days. Every morning, he would plead with his mother to go see Arshaluys and make sure she was looked after.

Returning home, Mrs. Medzarian would buoy him but could say nothing definite about Arshaluys' condition.

"So she won't come by tomorrow either?" Ara would ask.

73

"I don't know, son."

Sometimes, in order to make Ara forget his disappointment, Mrs. Medzarian would signal Satenig to cheer him up. The girl would jump and sit on her brother's lap and goof around.

Ara would press his kid sister's head to his chest. "You're my little joy, you crazy girl," he'd say.

Three days had passed since Ara had last heard Arshaluys' voice in his deathly-silent room. In the evening, when his mother came to see how he was doing, he asked her: "Isn't there church service anymore?"

"No, son, the priest was exiled."

"And the church?"

"Well, it's been closed because the congregation has been driven away." She thought it wise not to tell him about the massacres that had followed the community's deportation.

"What about our beloved eagles?" Ara asked. "Do they still live on top of the rocks?"

"Not anymore, son. They either died or flew away."

"And our cemetery?"

"It's still there," Mrs. Medzarian half-lied, as she knew the Turks had desecrated and destroyed the entire site.

"I'm bored, mom," Ara said. "Let's go to the cemetery. Lately I've been wanting to say the Lord's Prayer on grandpa's grave."

Mrs. Medzarian objected. She told him it was already dark and cold outside. But Ara wouldn't hear any of it. At last she relented.

Covering their heads with black shawls, Mrs. Medzarian and Satenig led Ara to the cemetery.

They proceeded like shadows through the streets, under a pale moon-light. Mrs. Medzarian was terrified of the possibility of coming face to face with a Turkish acquaintance, who perhaps would follow them and discover the real purpose of their outing. After all, their lives had been spared through a supreme act of compassion on the part of the Turks. Furthermore, they had been allowed to accept Islam, whereas what they were engaged in tonight, namely going to visit the Armenian cemetery, would clearly be deemed by their Turkish benefactors a sacrilege of the most odious kind. Fortunately the few villagers they encountered didn't seem in the least curious about them.

When they reached the cemetery, towering poplars cast immense

shadows across the ground, which was strewn with smashed tombstones sleeping in complacent peace. As the tree leaves made plaintive songs with their monotonous rustle, the dead, too, slept serenely, in a contentment which was denied to their tombless sons and daughters, all those who had been butchered or died of hunger on the roads of deportation.

The sharp hoot of an owl made Satenig clutch her mother's skirt. "I'm scared, mom," she said, closing her eyes.

Making the sign of the cross, Mrs. Medzarian turned to Ara. "Go ahead, son, say the Lord's Prayer," she said. "It's chilly out here. We should go back."

"No, not yet," Ara said decisively. "Take me to grandfather's grave. I've got a lot to tell him."

The ground was all but impassable. Overgrown grass, heaps of earth, and innumerable fragments of broken headstones made it difficult for the night pilgrims to advance. The blind young man's cane often struck pieces of stone, with the bangs reverberating against the eerie silence, like doleful wake-up calls directed at the dead.

They came to a stop beneath a familiar poplar. Mrs. Medzarian had not been there since the start of the atrocities. She watched in horror the overturned and broken tombstones of family members.

"Here it is, son, grandpa's grave," she said.

With childlike sprightliness, Ara fumbled around until he found the poplar, then put his arms around its rough trunk, as though measuring its thickness.

"Yes, this is it," he whispered.

He took three steps forward and used his cane to grope for something in the empty space. Failing to find it, he stood still, perplexed.

"Mother," he said, "I know this place well. Grandpa's gravestone should've been right here..."

After a deep sigh, Mrs. Medzarian decided it would be pointless to continue the charade. She held his cold hands and stroked them, then said, "Don't be sad, son. The savages left nothing of our sanctities. They knocked down our gravestones and shattered our crosses. Look, your grandfather's overturned gravestone is right in front of you."

"Yes, I see it," Ara said. "I see that smashed red granite cross lying among the wild grass. I see that headstone, over there, that's been broken into pieces. And I see the bare graves lying flat on the ground, without their headstones, nettles sprouting all around them..."

Satenig and her mother listened in amazement. How precisely he described the scene! Did he actually see the ruins of the cemetery?

"Can you see, Ara?" Satenig asked. "Can you really see?"

"I can; I always have," he said.

Eaglet now hovered above his grandfather's felled tombstone. He bent over and stroked its hefty torso. He had always worshipped his granddad. It was he who had first kindled Ara's imagination when he was a child, and gone on to give everything he had to make sure that his grandson received the best possible education in Istanbul.

Ara stroked his grandfather's tombstone for several minutes, gauging with his hands the enormity of the wreckage. Then he knelt and let out a cry, in the heart-rending tone of a drowning man: "Forgive me, grandfather. My arms are unable, forever unable, to rebuild your tomb and take revenge for your dishonor."

***

The autumn rains frequently flooded the village, shrouding it in a patina of gloom.

Soon after Arshaluys' husband got well and once again left on business, she resumed her visits to the Medzarians.

Ara felt alive, electrified by a renewed sense of purpose.

In the course of the past five months, by overhearing many conversations at home, especially those with visiting Turkish neighbors, he had learned of the tragedies that had befallen the village and his loved ones. The only thing about which he continued to be in the dark was the matter of the woman he loved. Specifically, two mysteries kept him awake at night: how had Arshaluys and her mother managed to survive the slaughter of the Armenian community and permitted to remain in the village? And considering the fact that Arshaluys' mother allowed her to freely visit him, why didn't she herself come by to say hello, at least once?

These were questions he puzzled over unceasingly, and which Arshaluys had made a habit of answering with a well-timed kiss, before he had a chance to pose them.

One day, during a fierce downpour, Arshaluys ran in, soaked from head to toe. She spent the whole day with the Medzarians. Everyone was in high spirits. Ara kept running his fingers through Arshaluys' hair, playing childish games.

As soon as the rain stopped, he asked her to accompany him to the garden. She didn't think twice. She took his arm and they headed out, prancing friskily.

She placed a blanket on a chair and they sat down glued to one another, clasping hands. He had never felt this happy.

He thought therefore that the moment was ripe to ask her the big question, hoping she would at last give him the answer he lived for.

She, on the other hand, could not have been more removed from his state of mind.

The eventuality which she had dreaded for the past several months was already upon her. Her husband had asked the authorities to transfer his practice to a big city. His request was approved, and a week ago he had written Arshaluys, asking her to pack whatever she could and leave town on the forthcoming Wednesday, together with their housemaid, to join him in the city. As for their furniture and other belongings, he had asked some Turkish friends, Ali Efendi and his wife, to sell them for him at their leisure.

Ever since reading her husband's letter, Arshaluys had been unable to sleep, often sobbing out of sheer helplessness. To escape, yes. But where? And how? True, her only hope, her ultimate haven, was a mere holler away from her, yet he was a man stripped of his eyesight, someone whose wings had been clipped, turning him into a grave of the rebellious soars of his dreams.

Her life no longer meant anything to her. All that remained to do was make the supreme sacrifice for her unfortunate lover. That is to say, to escape to his home and refuse to leave until the Turks dragged her corpse out... or to commit suicide, at least so as to leave Eaglet with the memory of an undying love.

At the end, neither seemed a good option. Both would serve only to destroy the young man, physically and emotionally. Besides, the revelation of her secret alone — the fact that she had been sharing the bed of a Turk — would be enough to shatter Ara.

The previous night, once again unable to sleep, Arshaluys had at last decided on a course of action. She would spend her last day in town at her lover's home; she would act cheerful and reiterate her promises of everlasting devotion; but then she would break the news, as gently as she knew how, telling Ara that she and her mother had resolved to leave town the following morning and go live with some Islamized relatives in the city, for economic and physical survival, in view of the ongoing atrocities committed against the Armenians.

Thus the lovers, unaware of the storm which raged inside the other, sat shoulder to shoulder in the garden, listening to the drips of raindrops which fell on dead leaves every time Ara's fidgety legs hit against the tree trunk.

Both felt that the time had come to open up in earnest. Yet the words they needed to say remained frozen in their throats. Instead they exchanged trivial comments about the leaves and the setting sunset and the wind.

Suddenly a prodigious lightning shot through the sky, followed by a terrifying thunder that rumbled across the valley. The lovers hugged instinctively.

"Arshaluys, take pity on me," he entreated. "All I want is a ray of hope from you. And only you. I'm exhausted... Please don't go away anymore..."

It was at that instant that Arshaluys suddenly realized she was running late. Ali Efendi and his wife must've already arrived at her house to sort out their goods and help her pack up for her trip the next morning. Certainly her absence would rouse suspicions, and her husband's friends were sure to organize a search party to find her.

While these images were sinking in and she felt with every fiber of her body the boundless suffering of the pleading boy, she knew she had to put an end to the deceit.

She went on to deal the fateful, ruthless blow.

"Give up on me already, Ara," she snapped, with a brisk move to disentangle herself from his arms.

"No, Arshaluys! Without you I'm nothing. Please don't go."

"I'm out of time, Ara," she said. "My mother is waiting for me. Take care of yourself. Tomorrow we'll be leaving town... But your memory will forever be sealed in my heart."

"You'll be leaving? Why? No, don't say that."

Her last words were barely audible. "Farewell, Ara," she said. "Farewell, my love. My life will be nothing but darkness from now on."

With this, Arshaluys rushed off and within a second vanished into the stormy night.

He was whirling, disoriented, unable to make sense of what had just happened.

He lost his balance and fell face down into the washtub, letting out a howl of powerless rage.

As they ran to the garden, his mother, grandmother, and sister found him lying in the tub, his glasses thrown off his maimed eyelids, and a stream of tears flowing down his cheeks.

"Ara, come to your senses, my child," his mother implored him, kneeling down next to him. "Come on, get up, say something, move around."

He didn't react.

"Ara, take pity on us!" Mrs. Medzarian now screamed. "Don't you see our misfortune, son? Don't you see?"

"I became blind, mother," he said after a while. "I don't see anymore."

1918

Other publications
of the Genocide Library

Volume 1
Passage through Hell: A Memoir
- The Odyssey of a Genocide Survivor -
by **Armen Anush**
(First Edition: 2005, Second Edition: 2007)

Volume 2
The Fatal Night: An Eyewitness Account
of the Extermination of Armenian Intellectuals in 1915
by **Mikayel Shamtanchian**
(2007)

Volume 3
Death March: An Armenian Survivor's Memoir
of the Genocide of 1915
by **Shahen Derderian**
(2008)

Volume 4
The Crime of the Ages: A Chronicle
of Turkey's Genocide of the Armenians
by **Sebuh Aguni**
(2010)

Volume 5
Defying Fate: The Memoirs of
Aram and Dirouhi Avedian
(2014)

For inquiries and orders, write to:
H. and K. Manjikian Publications
P. O. Box 2734, Toluca Lake, California 91610-0734